The British Economy

An Elementary Macroeconomic Perspective

SECOND EDITION

M.H. PESTON

Queen Mary College, University of London

Philip Allan

First published 1982 by

PHILIP ALLAN PUBLISHERS LIMITED
MARKET PLACE
DEDDINGTON
OXFORD OX5 4SE

Second edition 1984

British Library Cataloguing in Publication Data

Peston, M.H.
   The British economy.—2nd ed.
   1. Macroeconomics   2. Great Britain—
   Economic policy—1945-
   I. Title
   339'.0941   HC256.6

   ISBN 0-86003-059-8
   ISBN 0-86003-165-9 Pbk

Set by M H L Typesetting Limited, Coventry
Printed and bound in Great Britain by
The Camelot Press Limited, Southampton

The British Economy

An Elementary Macroeconomic Perspective

Contents

Introduction   1

1   National Income   6

2   Changes in Income   15

3   Consumer Spending, Saving and Investment   25

4   Unemployment   45

5   Inflation   58

6   The Balance of Payments   79

7   Money   96

8   Public Expenditure and Taxation   109

9   Growth   123

10 Some Conclusions   142

Appendix I   148

Appendix II   163

Index   165

Introduction

Macroeconomics is the study of the economy as a whole. Typical macroeconomic theory is set out in terms of aggregates such as total unemployment or the sum of all incomes earned in a country. It also concerns itself with such averages as the index of retail prices or the index of money wages. To put the point differently, the macroeconomist studies the behaviour of firms as a whole or households as a whole while the microeconomist concentrates on the theory of the individual firm or the individual household. Yet another way of making the point is to say that the macroeconomist simplifies his account of the economy to concentrate on the following markets:

(i) the market for goods and services
(ii) the market for labour
(iii) the market for money and other financial assets

This is a simplification because in the real world there are many markets for goods and services, for factors of production, and for assets. Nonetheless, abstraction and simplification are part and parcel of the scientific method, and it is, of course, possible to derive conclusions relevant to reality from theories which are themselves some distance from it.

Elementary macroeconomic theory concentrates on the national economy. It does this, initially, by totally ignoring the rest of the world. Since, however, all markets involve transactions of an international nature, slightly more advanced theory must take account of foreign trade, and of foreign financial matters. (It should be added that in some economies, at some times, international movement of labour also requires explicit discussion.)

Despite the focus on the national economy, other units, both larger and smaller are worth noting. There is an emerging field of world macroeconomics, and, perhaps, one day there will even be an intergalactic side of the subject! More seriously, there can certainly be a macroeconomics of an international bloc such as the EEC. At a less aggregated level, it is obvious that there can be a macroeconomic study of a region of a country, e.g. the North West of England, or the lowlands of Scotland.

The problems of macroeconomics can be stated in a straightforward fashion. Modern macroeconomics started with the major concern with unemployment that dominated thinking in Great Britain in the 1920s and 1930s. The theoretical breakthrough here was attributable to Keynes, and is often called the Keynesian revolution. While there is no doubt that there was a Keynesian revolution, and that Keynes was the leading economist of his generation, it is worth knowing that he was not alone in contributing to our understanding of the subject. Economics in the 1930s was in a lively state, and many other economists at home and overseas had important things to say. (Special mention must be made of the great Polish economist, Kalecki, who was at the very least an independent discoverer of what is called Keynesian theory.)

Unemployment was the dominant problem of the 1930s and is so today. It was, and is, regarded as a social evil, and as something likely to imperil the very existence of parliamentary democracy, if it becomes chronic. Unemployment has been characteristic of what is called industrial capitalism and goes back to the beginning of the 19th century. (Curiously enough the word itself came later, not emerging until well into the 19th century.)

An old problem of macroeconomics was that of inflation, the tendency for prices on average to rise for quite long periods of time. Attempts to understand inflation go back to the sixteenth and seventeenth centuries. Indeed, it may be said that inflation was the first problem of macroeconomics, if not of economics altogether. (It may be added, incidentally, that there are economists who think that our understanding of inflation has scarcely improved since that time!)

A related problem of similar antiquity is about the balance of trade. A country buying more from foreigners than they buy from us must run down its assets abroad, or borrow abroad, or pay for the difference in some currency acceptable to them. The last did include (and still does to some extent) paying in gold. For three or four hundred years there have been debates on the importance of the overseas trade account, and the desirability of accumulating gold and foreign assets. More recently, the debate has also focused on how adverse trends in external trade may inhibit the proper working of the home economy. The issue here used to be put as one of the balance of payments acting as a constraint on improved UK economic performance. It might be argued, with equal correctness, that it is poor UK economic performance that allowed the balance of payments to be an inhibiting factor.

A key measure of economic performance that has dominated economic discussion for the past thirty years has been economic growth. As a matter of fact, UK economic growth since the Second World War was faster (at least up to the mid-1970s) than in any earlier period of similar length. Nonetheless, other countries improved their efficiency at an even faster rate. This provided a kind of crisis for UK policy makers in the 1960s and early 1970s. An attempt to explain growth joined the other parts of macroeconomics, and may even have dominated them for a while.

It is worth adding that what is considered the central issue does change over time. Growth may have dominated the 1960s, even swamping unemployment as the centre of attention, largely because the problem of the latter was thought to be solved. In the 1970s, inflation took the centre of the stage. In the 1980s, unemployment is becoming the dominant issue again, while growth prospects are seen as rather dim.

A main theme of what follows is how the concerns of macroeconomics changed in the 1970s. To that must be added two other matters. Macroeconomics itself is developing rapidly. It is a long time since so much first-class theoretical work has been undertaken in this area. That is connected with an extremely lively debate on the fundamentals of the way the economy works. Connected with it has been a deep pessimism over the future of the economy and the possibility of using economic policy to help the system work more satisfactorily.

Macroeconomics has always been a policy science. It tries to explain how the economy works, but it is also interested in the investigation (and invention) of tools to make it work better. Up to the mid-1970s it is not too much to say that economists were pretty confident that they knew enough about how the system worked to be able to advise governments about what to do if inflation or unemployment became too high, or growth slackened, or the balance of payments became adverse. They believed they knew which instruments would be effective, and the policy problem was one of using them at the right time and on the correct scale.

Now, economists are not so sure. They have not gone to the other extreme of deep despair, of saying nothing can be done. But most of them are more cautious in giving advice, and see the path to better days as a difficult and very slow one.

With that background, the purpose of this short book is to act as an adjunct to the economic theory set out in the main textbooks. That theory is expressed admirably, but is often at some distance from the actual problems that gave rise to it. It may be added that, in the opinion of the present writer, the best available textbooks are pretty well all from the USA. This means that their factual content and emphasis is not appropriate for the UK.

Apart from supplementing the theory, however, this book has two other objectives. One is to emphasise the real problems, so that the reader can start to appreciate what the purpose of the theory is. Related to this is the hope that the economics student will see the importance of arguing for himself, and of not taking things on trust just because they are in a textbook. Secondly, reality for the economist is shown to a large extent (but not wholly) in published statistics. Even the most elementary student must get into the habit of using them. Much can be learned simply by tabulating the figures and plotting them on graphs and scatter diagrams. Without decrying econometric methods, they can be rather mechanical and unenlightening. A simpler, yet still quantitative, approach can be enlightening, can uncover important issues, and can subsequently motivate the use of econometric techniques.

This leads to our last objective. The student must be critical of all that he is taught, and above all must ask the question 'how do I discover whether or not this proposition is true?' In a deep sense we are unable to test theories in this elementary account of the subject, or to describe the equivalent of crucial experiments. We do try and show, however, how hard it is to discover truth in economic science, or to choose between seemingly irreconcilable views of the way the economy works.

It is to be hoped that the student imbued with the critical spirit will turn on the book itself. It contains much that is problematic and some things which are certainly wrong. The trouble is that I do not know which those parts are, but will be delighted to hear from anyone who is sure he can spot truth from falsehood!

I must thank all those of my former students who have discussed macroeconomics with me for many years now. I have learned much from them and hope that they have benefited, at least to a moderate extent, from the economics teaching at Queen Mary College. Since so many of them have risen in the world of economics, and quite a few teach the subject to even later generations, I hope that they spotted my many errors in good time, and allowed for them.

Finally, I must thank E.C.R. Peston whose critical comments and advice have made this a better book than would otherwise have been the case.

This second edition has brought the relevant statistics up to date to include 1982. I have eliminated a number of errors. I wish to thank John Black in particular, for drawing many of these to my attention.

1
National Income

Money national income consists of all the income received by the inhabitants of a country in a period of time (say, a year). Most of this income is received in return for economic activity in the country itself, and may be called domestic income. Some, however, is received as a return on capital invested abroad.

Since income is received for economic activity, we can also start from the other end, so to speak, and consider the value of goods and services sold in a year. This value of what he sells minus what he paid to produce it accrues directly to the seller as income. But what he paid to produce it is what someone else sells to him. They, in the same way, will regard that (net of costs) as income. This calculation can continue until the value of the initial sale is fully attributed to someone as income. The value of what is produced and sold in a country is called the *gross domestic product* (GDP), and by our argument is equal to the domestic part of money national income. If we add the income earned abroad to the *gross domestic product*, the resulting figure is called the *gross national product* (GNP).

We have referred to the receipts of the seller from which he deducts his costs to obtain his income. Many sellers are, of course, firms. The income received will be that of the owner-manager, i.e. it will be a combination of salary and profits. It may, however, be simply a matter of profits accruing to the owners of the firm, management receiving a salary along with other employees. This reminds us that many of the sellers in the economy (actually more than 23 million of

6

them) are individuals who are selling labour services, mostly to firms, but occasionally directly to the general public. It should also be borne in mind that economic activity requires the use of land and buildings, the owners of which receive an income called rent.

We may, therefore, divide the income received into the following:

(i)   income from employment, i.e. in broad terms, wages and salaries
(ii) income from self-employment, e.g. the smaller shop-keeper, accountants, etc.
(iii) profits
(iv) rent

These are what may be called functional categories of income. It follows that one person may have more than one source of income. A person may work in one firm, have shares in another, and also own part of a building hired by a third firm. In this case, he has three categories of income. Most ordinary people, although they have to rely overwhelmingly on employment income, do have some savings which might be in a unit trust or invested in a pension fund, and, therefore, receive an additional return.

Reverting to our main theme, it was said that what the seller received was kept by him or paid to some other seller. In the case of firms, however, there is another consideration to take into account. The government levies taxes on expenditure (or indirect taxes), notably VAT and the customs and excise duties, on goods that are sold. It also subsidises some producers and sellers. The prices at which goods are sold are called their *market prices*. If from these prices are deducted expenditure taxes and to them are added subsidies, the resulting figure (times the quantity sold) is what accrues to the factors of production which produced the good in question. Prices net of expenditure taxes and subsidies are called *factor costs*. (It should be pointed out that the scale of taxes on expenditure is some eight times that of subsidies so that market prices exceed factor costs.)

The value of goods and services actually sold is called the *gross domestic product at market prices*. The value of

Table 1.1 National Income for 1982, £m.

I.	Gross Domestic Product at Market Prices	274,183
II.	Gross National Product at Market Prices	275,760
III.	Gross Domestic Product at Factor Cost	232,553
IV.	Gross National Product at Factor Cost	234,130
V.	National Income	201,073

goods and services actually sold, minus taxes on expenditure plus subsidies, is called the *gross domestic product at factor cost*. (A similar point applies to gross national product.)

Lastly, we must explain the meaning of 'gross'. During the production process some capital equipment is used up, in the sense that it gets nearer the end of its life, or needs servicing to keep it going. In other words, production involves *capital consumption*. If the income of owners of capital is meant to measure how well off they are, it is obviously necessary to deduct capital consumption from what they actually receive. If capital consumption is deducted from gross national product, the resulting figure is called *net national product* or *national income*.

The actual figures for 1982 are given in Table 1.1. From these figures it is possible to infer

(i)   Net property income from abroad — II minus I
(ii)   The adjustment for factor cost — I minus III
(iii) Capital consumption — IV minus V.

The division of factor incomes is given in Table 1.2.

Table 1.2 Division of Factor Incomes for 1982, £m.

I.	Income from employment	155,133
II.	Income from self-employment	20,068
III.	Gross trading profits of companies	33,344
IV.	Gross trading profits of public corporations and enterprises	9,192
V.	Rent	16,166
VI.	Other	-1,350
VII.	Gross Domestic Product at Factor Cost	232,553

Note: Category VI includes a whole host of minor items and adjustments irrelevant to our main theme.

Having explained what we mean by national income and national product, it may be asked what is the significance of these terms? What does it matter that GDP at factor cost was £232,553m. in 1982 rather than some other number? The answer is already apparent in the way we explained the terms. National income or gross domestic product is a measure of the scale of economic activity, and a great deal of economics is concerned with questions of why aggregate economic activity is at one level rather than another, and why it varies over time. Virtually everything in the remainder of this book is devoted, directly or indirectly, to explaining the cause of these variations.

Our discussion of terms also enables us to emphasise a distinction of vital importance to a proper understanding of macroeconomics. Reference has been made to the quantity of goods and services sold and the prices received for them. Equally, we have mentioned individual people's incomes which, multiplied by the number of people, gives national income.

Starting from the product side, gross domestic product may change because the quantities of goods and services produced and sold change, or because the prices at which these transactions occur, change. Usually both changes will occur, but not necessarily in the same direction.

On the incomes side, by similar reasoning, national income will change if the incomes received by individual factors of production change, or the number of factors of production receiving those incomes changes. Here, again, there is no reason why the movement of the two parts should always be in the same direction.

It is reasonable to argue, therefore, that gross domestic product changes because prices change on average or because quantities change on average. We may also say that national income changes because factor prices change on average or because employment (of factors of production) changes on average.

If gross domestic product is measured in such a way that the change in prices is taken out, it is referred to as *gross domestic product in real terms.* Comparing two periods of

Table 1.3 Gross Domestic Product for 1972 and 1982, £m.

	1972	1982	Percentage Change
Gross Domestic Product at Current Market Prices	63,774	274,183	330
Gross Domestic Product at Current Factor Cost	55,672	232,553	318
Gross Domestic Product at 1980 Market Prices	198,747	229,251	15
Gross Domestic Product at 1980 Factor Cost	172,199	198,324	15

time, the quantities of both are multiplied by the prices of one. As an example, gross domestic product may be evaluated in any year at the prices ruling in (say) 1980. It is for that reason that *gross domestic product in real terms* is also known as *gross domestic product at constant prices* (as opposed to gross domestic product at current prices). Moreover, those constant prices may be constant market prices or constant factor cost.

In Table 1.3 we show for the years 1972 and 1982 some of these figures. In the last column of this table we give the percentage change between the two years. Recall that we stated that the figure in constant prices (or real terms) was equal to the figure in current prices divided by an average price level. This means that, if we know GDP in both constant and current prices, we can divide the former into the latter to give an estimate of the level of average prices. Moreover, the difference between the percentage change in GDP at current prices and constant prices measures the change in the average level of prices.

In terms of Table 1.3 in the decade 1972-82, GDP at current market prices rose by 330% and at 1980 market prices by 15%. The difference between the two is indicative of the increase in average prices over the decade.

Thus, having started with an interest in measuring real economic activity by looking, for example, at the quantity of goods produced, we are led to the second major area of interest to economists, the average level of prices and the rate of inflation. The two are closely connected, a theme to which we return many times.

Let us for the moment go right back to the beginning in order to mention another aspect of income and economic activity, namely the categories of goods which are bought and sold. In addition, we must take note of the fact that not everybody spends all his income, but many save some. Others may spend more still and 'dissave'. Firms, in particular, may borrow in order to finance their capital investments. It is also necessary at this stage to mention another distinction, namely that between the public and private sectors. The government and local authorities engage in economic activity, employing people and buying goods and services from the private sector to provide public services. There are also the nationalised industries producing and selling goods and services.

Of all the goods and services produced in an economy, the following is what may happen to them:

(a)   They may be sold to private consumers at home;
(b)   They may be sold as consumer goods to the government;
(c)   They may be sold as capital goods to the private sector;
(d)   They may be sold as capital goods to the public sector;
(e)   They may be added to stock;
(f)   They may be sold abroad.

Of all the goods bought in the economy, some may be the result of domestic production, but some may come from abroad. Thus, total consumer expenditure equals that part produced at home (category (a) of the previous paragraph) plus that part imported from abroad. If, therefore, we write down all the categories of expenditure by residents of the country (households, firms, government, etc.), we get total final expenditure. In order to estimate gross domestic product, however, we must deduct from total final expenditure its import content.

In Table 1.4 we give the figures for the various categories of expenditure (which include an import element), and then deduct imports of goods and services to get the gross domestic product.

Table 1.4 Categories of Expenditure at Market Prices for 1982, £m.

Consumers' Expenditure	167,128
General Government Final Consumption	60,082
Gross Domestic Fixed Capital Formation:	42,172
(a) Private	30,491 }
(b) Public	11,681
Value of the Physical Increase in Stocks	−1,162
Exports of Goods and Services	73,128
Total Final Expenditure	341,348
Imports of Goods and Services	−67,165
Gross Domestic Product at Market Prices	274,183

Our earlier remarks on the distinction between current and constant prices also, of course, apply to the components of national income and expenditure. In Table 1.5 we give the same categories as in Table 1.4 but at 1980 prices.

We can now do, for each category of expenditure, the kind of calculation we did earlier for expenditure as a whole. This would enable us to partition the change in expenditure into a real or quantity component and a price component. To illustrate that in Table 1.6 we do the calculation just for a couple of components, namely consumer expenditure and imports.

Table 1.5 Categories of Expenditure at 1980 Market Prices for 1982, £m;

Consumers' Expenditure	138,865
General Government Final Consumption	49,011
Gross Domestic Fixed Capital Formation:	37,614
(a) Private	27,396 }
(b) Public	10,218
Value of the Physical Increase in Stocks	−1,031
Exports of Goods and Services	62,789
Total Final Expenditure	287,248
Imports of Goods and Services	−57,997
Gross Domestic Product at 1980 Market Prices	229,251

Table 1.6 Some GDP Components at Current and 1980 Market Prices, £m.

	1972	1982	Percentage Change
Consumers' Expenditure at Current Market Prices	40,500	167,128	313
Consumers' Expenditure at 1980 Market Prices	121,519	138,865	14
Imports at Current Market Prices	13,772	67,165	388
Imports at 1980 Market Prices	47,101	57,997	23

From these we obtain, as a rough approximation, an implicit increase of consumer goods prices of 299% and of import prices of 365%. Note that these are not the same as the increase of prices in general, which was 315%. We are thus led to another major preoccupation of economists which will be elaborated below, the significance of the change in relative prices. How important is it, for example, that between 1972 and 1982 the prices of consumer goods rose at an annual rate of 14% while the price of imports rose by 15% per annum?

There are many other aspects of national income which are important and which will be mentioned in due course. There is, however, one which can be explained right away. Although a household, for example, receives or is entitled to an income, it is not able to dispose of all of that. One reason is that the government takes away from the household such direct taxes as income tax and national insurance. A second is that the household may be a part owner of a firm, but may not receive all the profit made to which it is entitled as a dividend. Some may be retained in the firm (as a precaution or to help to finance capital investment). It should also be noted on the other side of the scale that some household receipts are not income for economic activity. Households receive transfer payments from the government in the form of pensions, child benefits, unemployment pay etc. The gross receipts of households, including these transfer payments, is

Table 1.7 Personal Incomes for 1982, £m.

	Income from Employment	155,133
Plus	Income from Self-Employment	20,068
Plus	Other Income	26,223
Plus	Transfer Payments	36,519
Equals	Personal Income	237,943
Less	Taxes, National Insurance etc.	50,641
Gives	Personal Disposable Income	187,302
	Consumers' Expenditure	167,128
	Saving	20,174

called *personal income*. Making the deductions we have referred to leads to what is called *personal disposable income*. The figures are given in Table 1.7.

We have also added to that table household expenditure on consumer goods and services. The difference between that and personal disposable income is defined as the saving of the personal sector.

Questions

1. What do we mean by 'economic activity'?

2. Are there examples of economic activity that are not included in national income?

3. Many more married women now go to work than did in the 1960s. How does this affect the interpretation of national income?

4. Saving by households is defined as their disposable income minus their expenditure on consumer goods and services. Is this definition satisfactory? In criticising it, consider the different types of consumer goods that are bought. Consider also whether the *form* in which saving takes place is important.

5. Does national income in constant prices measure a country's standard of living?

2
Changes in Income

In this chapter we intend to see how United Kingdom national income has changed over time. For the most part we shall concentrate on the 1970s, but because of the contrast we shall make some remarks on the experience of the previous decade, that of the 1960s, and on the current decade, the 1980s.

In Figure 2.1 we plot the path of gross domestic product at current prices and at 1980 prices. The former shows a continuous, and, if anything, accelerating upward trend. But in itself, as we have already said, that does not mean very much. A more suitable measure of the scale of economic activity and its growth is given by GDP at constant prices. (Note that this lies above the current price line before 1980 and below it after 1980. The reason is the obvious one that the actual price level has been rising continuously over time. Thus, the output of years before 1980 is revalued at higher prices than actually ruled, and after 1980 at lower prices.)

GDP at constant prices, or real GDP, also has an upward trend, but much less than that of GDP at current prices. It also fluctuates more, and on two occasions, 1973—5 and 1979—81, actually falls.

An examination of the graph suggests that average growth was fairly steady up to about the beginning of the 1970s. From about 1973 onwards, however, growth appears to slacken. In fact, the average growth rate from 1958 to 1973 was just about 3% per annum. If real output had continued to grow at that rate on average through the rest of the 1970s it would have stood at about £267,000m. in 1983, some 15% above the level it actually reached.

15

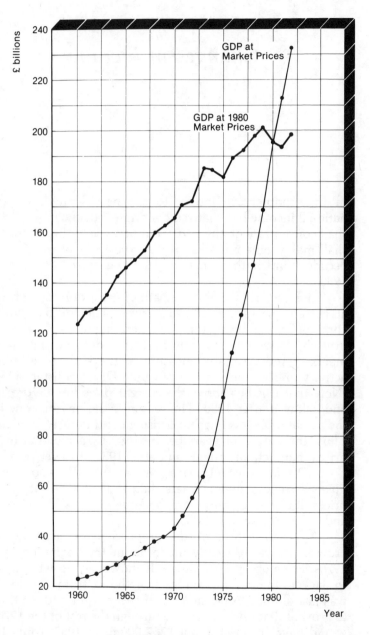

Figure   2.1

In other words, it looks as if in the 1970s something happened to reduce our real growth rate. It has been suggested that this may have been connected with the rise in price of oil and of energy in general, or the increased inflation rate, or simply the exhaustion of potential improvements in productive efficiency. We return to this in Chapter 9 but before doing so must look more closely at what has happened over the longer period to output and prices.

In Table 2.1 we show the annual percentage changes of GDP at current prices and constant prices. From 1959-69 money income increased each year by between about 5% and 9%, while real output increased by between 1% and 5%. The average rate of increase in money income was 6.7%, and of real income 3.2%. Thus both money and real income fluctuated about their mean levels by plus or minus 2%. Although it can be argued endlessly about what degree of fluctuation is to be called stability, it can surely be agreed that these variations are not very large. Whether that is attributable to an inherent stability in the economy or whether it was the result of active policy is debatable.

It is argued in economic theory that private investment and exports fluctuate causing the economy to follow suit. This may be offset by variations in public expenditure in the opposite direction, or taxes in the same direction. The first of these adds directly to effective demand when it would otherwise be low, or subtracts from it when it might be high. The second allows consumption expenditure to vary inversely with exports and investment. Alternatively, expansionary monetary policy and a low interest rate might cause private expenditure to rise when that is needed, and contractionary policy cause it to fall in opposite circumstances.

It might be thought, therefore, that it is easy to see whether policy helped to stabilise the economy. All that needs to be done is to compare changes in private expenditure with changes in public expenditure and taxation while also allowing for monetary effects. Unfortunately, matters are not as easy as that. One reason is the matter of timing. If private investment falls, it would take time for the government to recognise that and act. Also, if its response is less than

Table 2.1 Percentage Changes in GDP at Constant and Current Prices

	(a) Percentage Change of GDP at 1980 Market Prices	(b) Pecentage Change of GDP at Current Market Prices	(c) (b) − (a)
1959	3.9	5.3	1.4
1960	4.8	5.8	1.0
1961	3.4	7.1	3.7
1962	1.0	4.7	3.7
1963	4.2	6.4	2.2
1964	5.2	9.1	3.9
1965	2.4	7.5	5.1
1966	1.9	6.6	4.7
1967	2.8	5.8	3.0
1968	4.2	8.5	4.3
1969	1.3	6.8	5.5
1970	2.2	9.7	7.5
1971	2.6	12.2	9.6
1972	2.2	10.6	8.4
1973	7.6	15.2	7.6
1974	−0.9	13.7	14.6
1975	−0.8	26.1	26.9
1976	3.7	19.2	15.5
1977	1.2	15.3	14.1
1978	3.5	15.0	11.5
1979	2.0	16.8	14.8
1980	−2.6	16.7	19.3
1981	−1.7	10.2	11.9
1982	1.9	9.7	7.8

perfect, public expenditure will still be rising when private investment is also rising. It follows that the facts will only show to a moderate degree an inverse relationship between public and private spending, even if the former is helping to offset changes in the latter. It is also worth considering that private expenditure itself stayed at a high level simply because households and firms expected the government to maintain effective demand at a high level and use the available policy weapons for stabilisation purposes.

Let us examine Table 2.1 now to see whether it throws any light on one or two other aspects of elementary economic theory. In the theory of the multiplier in its simplest form, the level of prices is assumed to be constant. It would then follow that money and real income (and expenditure) were the same thing. An increase in the one was equal to an increase in the other. Although that is a useful simplification for some purposes it clearly is not exactly true, since in every year in Table 2.1 the increase in money income exceeded the increase in real income (or, what amounts to the same thing, there was price inflation).

In fact, in slightly more advanced theory an upward-sloping aggregate supply curve is postulated. It then follows that, if effective demand in money or nominal terms increases by a given percentage, real demand and output will increase by a smaller percentage. It is, however, taken for granted that the output effect exceeds the price effect. In addition, implicit in the way the theory is used is the proposition that if nominal demand increases more, so will real demand.

Are both these propositions true in fact? An examination of the figures for 1959 to 1969 shows that the price effect and the output effect were of about the same order of magnitude. Actually, prices rose on average about 3.5% a year which is a little more than the 3.2% a year average rise in output. In other words, more than half the increase in nominal demand was dissipated in price rises even in that stable and allegedly non-inflationary era.

On the second proposition, it can be seen that it holds true in eight occasions out of ten. Only in 1961 (when nominal income grew more rapidly than in the previous year and real output grew less rapidly), and in 1967 (when the reverse happened) were there counter examples. Thus, it was moderately safe to use elementary macroeconomic theory in explaining the behaviour of the economy in the decade of the 1960s.

What of the past decade? Clearly, the rate of expansion of real output went down, and price inflation went up. Thus, although nominal income grew by an average of 15.4% each year, real output only grew by 1.4% annually. Some nine tenths of the increase in nominal income was dissipated in price rises.

Concerning the second proposition, that too holds less than in the 1960s. Five out of eleven occasions showed the wrong effect. In 1976, 1978, 1980 and 1982, nominal income grew less quickly and real income more quickly. Essentially, the last five years of the decade were when the new phenomenon, if that it is, appeared.

Another question that is worth asking is whether there is a positive or negative connection between the rate of increase in real output and the inflation rate. One view is that the faster nominal demand rises, the faster will real output rise and also, with greater pressure on available capacity, the more rapidly will prices go up. Thus, a positive connection between growth of prices and output would be expected. The reverse view is that, given the rise in nominal demand, the less rapidly prices rose, the more rapidly output would grow, and *vice versa*. In this version a negative relationship between growth of prices and output would be expected.

In this case, an examination of Table 2.1 shows that no clear-cut answer can be given. Of 23 observations, in ten cases the growth of real output and the inflation rate moved in the same direction, and in thirteen cases they moved in the opposite direction.

In Figure 2.2 an attempt is made to take this a little further. On the horizontal axis is plotted the percentage increase in GDP at constant prices and on the vertical axis the percentage increase in prices (or the inflation rate). Each point is an observation for a particular year and is identified as such. It appears, looking at this figure, that there was a negative relationship between these two variables in the 1960s, but a far from perfect one. (In fact, the correlation between the two is -0.56.) After that there is a shift and a possible new relationship appears in the period from 1973 onwards. It must be emphasised, however, that this really is problematic and it would be unwise to be too confident about what the data show. Moreover, even if there is something there, it is not clear-cut whether it is a more rapid rise in output that causes a lower inflation rate, or a lower inflation rate which causes a more rapid rise in output, or a third variable which determines the connection between the two, to the extent that it exists at all! It is also worth asking,

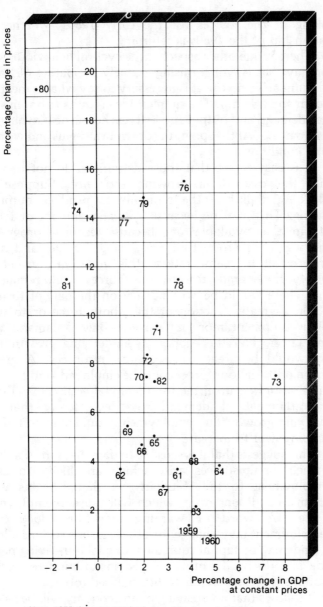

Note: 1975 data are not included; they lie outside this range.

Figure 2.2

looking at the figures for the early 1980s, whether the relationship of the 1960s is returning.

There is one other aspect of the cyclical behaviour of the economy that is worth raising, namely the dating of booms and slumps. To do this it is necessary to say what is meant by a boom and a slump. The simplest idea is that the boom starts when demand and output rise and reaches its peak when they cease to do so. At that point the downturn begins and we enter slump conditions.

It is easy to see that those definitions do not fit at all easily the case of a growing economy. Suppose the underlying ability of the economy to produce output is growing. This may be because a greater amount of labour and capital is available, and because technical progress is occurring and productivity is rising. If demand were increasing at the same rate as this *underlying growth of capacity*, the overall pressure on resources would remain the same. There would be no tendency on the part of firms to take on a greater fraction of the labour force or to work capital equipment more intensively. But, if demand were rising faster than the economy's underlying growth rate, there would be greater pressure on resources. A greater fraction of the labour force would be employed, and a similar change would occur in the use of capital equipment. By the same argument, if demand rose less slowly than the underlying growth rate, employment would start to fall and unemployment to increase.

This suggests that it is sensible to date the start of a boom as when circumstances arise which are likely to cause unemployment to fall. Similarly, a slump begins when economic conditions occur which will cause unemployment to rise. (A word of warning must be added here. Unemployment may change for other reasons such as a long-run tendency for capital equipment of a labour-saving nature to be introduced. In other words, in addition to cyclical variations there are trends to be analysed too.)

It follows that an upswing of an economy will be said to occur when output rises faster than the underlying growth rate. The boom then proceeds until output rises more slowly than the underlying growth rate when a downturn and slump ensue.

What then have been the boom and slump years of the UK economy? Let us try and answer this question by looking again at Table 2.1. Assume the underlying growth rate of the economy was about 3%. This means that a boom ended between the end of 1961 and the beginning of 1962, i.e. the percentage change in output dropped from 3.4% to 1.0%. This recession did not last long and there was an upturn in 1963 lasting two years, followed by a downturn in 1965. Viewed in this way, we would say that upturns occurred in 1963, 1968, 1973, 1976 and 1978, and downturns in 1961, 1965, 1969, 1974, 1977 and 1979. It is worth noting that the economy came close to an upturn in 1971. We must also remind ourselves that we showed that the underlying growth rate of the economy probably fell in the mid 1970s. If, for example, it was 2% or even 1.5%, that would still not affect the timing of most cycles. It would, however, affect our estimate of their *intensity*. The 3.7% expansion of 1976 is more powerful relative to a 2% underlying growth rate than to one of 3%. Also, if the growth rate benchmark is nearer 2% than 3%, not only would we regard 1971 as an upswing year but also 1982.

On the cycles themselves, there are three things to be said. Our method, though useful, is rather rough and ready. If we looked at quarter to quarter variations in output we might be able to date the cycles more precisely. Secondly, if the interval between cycles is taken to be the distance between successive downturns (or successive upturns), this is not a constant. The gaps between downturns are 4 years, 4 years, 5 years, 3 years, 2 years and 4 years. In other words, the cycles are not of precisely fixed duration. Thirdly, it might just about be argued that in the 1970s the cycles started to get shorter in magnitude than in the 1960s.

Questions

1.   What other economic variables might be examined to determine the extent of cycles in the economy?

2.   How would you expect the variability of real output measured quarterly to compare with real output measured annually?

3.   Suppose economic activity were divided into two parts;
      (i) manufacturing production, (ii) the remainder. Which
      would you expect to show faster longer term growth?
      Would you expect them to fluctuate to the same degree?

4.   Consider the timing of an upswing. Is it likely that all
      sectors of the economy would start to expand at the
      same time? If not, which would you expect to get started
      earlier? Would you expect the early starters also to be
      the early finishers, i.e. must it happen that a slump starts
      in the same part of the economy as a boom?

5.   In this chapter we have suggested that the more total
      demand rises, the more average prices rise. Is this view
      totally convincing? What arguments can you think of to
      lead you to the opposite opinion?

3
Consumer Spending, Saving and Investment

Elementary macroeconomic theory proceeds along the lines indicated by the presentation of the national income accounts in Chapter 1. It lays considerable emphasis on the components of national income, and on such matters as how consumer expenditure is determined by income, or how variations in investment or exports lead to variations in income.

The purpose of this chapter is to examine how some of the components of national income have changed over time. (Other components are dealt with in later chapters.) We shall look most closely at consumption, saving, and personal disposable income, on the one hand, and investment and stock building, on the other.

Consumers' expenditure comprises purchases by households of newly produced goods and services, some of which are durables (cars, refrigerators, television sets) which are not used up immediately in the period. Since not all consumer goods are perishable, consumers can add to their stock of these too. It follows that consumers' expenditure is not precisely the same thing as consumption, if that is taken to mean the using up of things. We shall concentrate on expenditure, and not worry too much about the distinction between that and consumption. We must recognise, however, that variations in purchase of consumer durables (including that most important durable of all, housing) are likely to be different from non-durables, and be influenced by some different forces. The most obvious factor is that of how easy it is to borrow and what interest has to be paid.

The basic proposition of macroeconomics is that real consumers' expenditure (i.e. expenditure in constant prices) is determined by real personal income. This is called the propensity to consume or consumption function. The figures are shown in Table 3.1. The data are also plotted in Figure 3.1.

What can we learn from this? Firstly, for the earlier part of the period up to 1973 disposable income rose in every year. While the rate of increase fluctuated, it was always positive. The same is true of real consumption expenditure. Secondly, there was some long-run tendency for consumption to rise less than disposable income. Since saving is *defined* as the difference between personal disposable income and consumption, what this means is that there was a tendency for the savings ratio to rise. This is shown in the last column. (The savings ratio is plotted against time in Figure 3.2.)

Thirdly, there were years in which consumption increased more than income. These were 1962, 1967, 1968, and 1971. On the whole those were years when income grew less rapidly compared with its average or normal path. This suggests that the short-run consumption function differs from the long-run function, and that changes in income which are assumed to be departures from the normal will lead to distinctly smaller changes in consumption. In other words, the savings ratio should peak in booms and fall in slumps. An examination of 1960, 1961, 1970, 1972, and 1973 gives some weight to that, as do the restrained years of 1962, 1967, 1968, and 1971. But the rise in the savings ratio of 1965, 1966, and 1969 remains a trifle puzzling.

Proceeding now to the 1970s, what stands out first of all are the years in which real personal disposable income and consumption fell. This was quite a new experience for the UK in contemporary times. Although fluctuations and inferior economic performance compared with foreign countries were recognised, affluence in the sense of continuing rising real incomes was taken for granted. This expectation was rudely shattered from 1974 onwards.

Next it is apparent that income was more volatile in the

Table 3.1 The Consumption Function

	Consumers' Expenditure at 1980 Prices		Personal Disposable Income at 1980 Prices		Savings ÷ Personal Disposable Income
	Level £bn*	Percentage Change	Level £bn*	Percentage Change	%
1958	80.9		83.9		4.0
1959	84.4	4.3	88.0	4.9	4.7
1960	87.7	3.9	93.3	6.0	6.6
1961	89.6	2.2	98.2	5.3	8.7
1962	91.7	2.3	98.9	0.7	7.5
1963	95.9	4.6	103.7	4.9	7.6
1964	98.8	3.0	107.4	3.6	8.2
1965	100.4	1.6	110.6	3.0	9.0
1966	102.2	1.8	112.7	1.9	9.4
1967	104.7	2.4	114.4	1.5	8.5
1968	107.8	3.0	116.3	1.7	7.4
1969	108.4	0.6	117.6	1.1	7.8
1970	111.2	2.6	122.2	3.9	9.0
1971	114.7	3.1	123.4	1.0	7.3
1972	121.5	5.9	134.6	9.1	9.7
1973	127.7	5.1	144.0	7.0	11.2
1974	125.6	−1.6	142.7	−0.9	12.0
1975	124.8	−0.6	142.8	0.0	12.5
1976	125.1	0.2	141.6	−0.8	11.7
1977	124.6	−0.4	139.3	−1.6	10.5
1978	131.5	5.5	149.7	7.5	12.1
1979	137.9	4.9	158.2	5.7	12.9
1980	136.9	−0.7	160.6	1.5	14.8
1981	137.1	0.1	156.6	−2.5	12.5
1982	138.9	1.3	155.6	−0.6	7.7

*Units are pounds billion, e.g. £42,100,000,000.

1970s than in the 1960s.Personal disposable income grew by 3.4% per annum in the 1960s and by 3.0% in the 1970s. In the former decade the actual changes per annum equalled the average plus or minus 2.5%. In the latter decade the range was plus or minus 5%. The range of variation just about

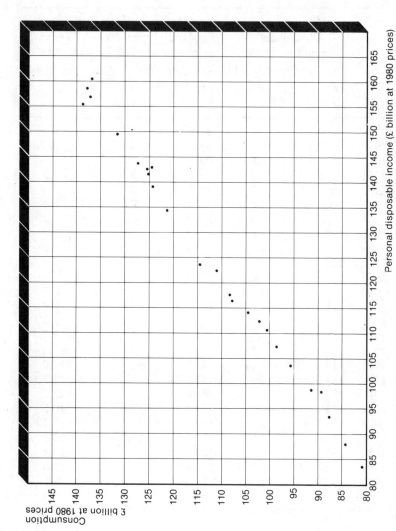

Figure 3.1

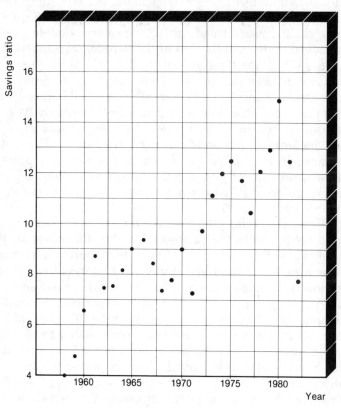

Figure 3.2

doubled. It is also true that the range of variation of consumers' expenditure rose significantly although not quite as much.

Thirdly, there was an extraordinary rise in the savings ratio. It had jumped in 1960 (signalling, perhaps, the end of the post-war era) and had then stayed in the range 7% to 9% with a slight upward trend. In 1973, it entered double figures and stayed there until the end of the decade, reaching 14.8% in 1980. What was the cause of this?

One answer lies in the great increase in disposable income in 1972 and 1973. This was the so-called Barber boom (after the then Chancellor of the Exchequer, Anthony Barber) and caused consumption to rise, but proportionately less than income as economic theory predicted. The ratio continued to rise in 1974 although income fell, and while it fell back subsequently, it did not return to its former level. The expansion of 1978 caused it to rise again and it continued upwards even in 1980.

Thus, the trend plus the two booms would lead us to expect some rise in the savings ratio, but the extent of the actual rise is rather surprising. One explanation that has been put forward is the volatility of incomes that has already been mentioned. People are more uncertain of what their incomes will be and save more as a precaution. Secondly, unemployment has risen considerably in the 1970s (a problem discussed in Chapter 4) and this too has added to people's anxiety about the future. (Some unemployed workers may also have temporarily saved their redundancy money.) Thirdly, there have been the higher inflation rates of the 1970s. These may be an extra factor in creating uncertainty and anxiety. Apart from that, it has been suggested that in inflationary conditions real money balances are eroded. The stock of money which people hold is part of their wealth. In conditions of greater inflation this is worth less in real terms (i.e. it can purchase less). It follows that in order to offset the decline in this part of their wealth, households save more. It has been suggested that the most recent savings figures are inaccurate anyway and exaggerate the increase in the propensity to save. (We discuss in Chapter 7 why people have tried to maintain their money balances given that their value falls more rapidly as inflation rises.) At the beginning of the 1980s the savings rate has fallen dramatically. This coincides with a drop in the inflation rate. Unemployment has remained high, but by 1983 appears to have become stabilised, at least for a time.

One other question that is worth asking about consumer expenditure and household disposable income concerns their relationship to the economy as a whole. Is consumption any less important today compared with ten and twenty years ago?

Table 3.2 GDP Ratios at Market Prices

	Consumers' Expenditure / GDP at Market Prices	Disposable Income / GDP at Market Prices
1962	0.67	0.72
1967	0.64	0.70
1972	0.64	0.70
1977	0.60	0.70
1982	0.61	0.68

In Table 3.2 we give the ratio of consumption to gross domestic product at market prices and personal disposable income to gross domestic product at market prices. It can be seen that there has been a decline in the relative importance of consumer expenditure in the economy as a whole. Moreover, since disposable income shows no great change relative to national income (up to the beginning of the 1980s, at which point there appears to have been a significant drop in the ratio of disposable income to GDP), the cause of this is the rise in the savings ratio. This will have been partially reversed by the consumer boom of 1983. (We return to the relationship between personal disposable income and national income in Chapter 8 where taxation and transfer payments are examined in more detail.)

We turn next to investment. In Table 3.3 we give the annual percentage change in gross domestic fixed capital formation at constant prices. This measures the increase in the stock of fixed assets available to the economy, but not

Table 3.3 Annual Percentage Change in Gross Domestic Fixed
Capital Formation (at constant prices)

	Private Sector	Government	Nationalised Industries	Total
1958				2.5
1959				6.1
1960				8.4
1961				10.5
1962				−1.0
1963	−3.5	−1.9	7.6	1.1
1964	15.8	16.4	11.2	14.6
1965	5.8	1.8	6.6	5.2
1966	−0.2	4.1	7.1	2.4
1967	1.9	14.9	13.7	7.6
1968	10.8	5.1	−6.5	4.5
1969	10.3	−1.4	−12.4	1.8
1970	5.3	8.6	3.8	5.8
1971	0.2	−1.3	1.2	0.5
1972	4.3	−2.6	−12.7	−0.8
1973	8.3	17.0	3.8	9.2
1974	−1.9	−11.1	14.5	−1.6
1975	−2.9	−13.0	8.6	−2.9
1976	3.4	−6.9	2.4	1.0
1977	8.4	−21.4	−7.7	−0.9
1978	11.0	−15.6	−4.8	3.7
1979	4.0	−0.2	−0.9	2.6
1980	−2.9	−15.9	−1.6	−4.1
1981	−5.4	−18.9	−5.3	−6.7
1982	8.8	−20.8	2.4	5.0

allowing for the fact that some of them wear out during the
year, or are getting nearer the end of their lives. This figure is
a mixed bag because it lumps together private and public
expenditure, and within the latter does not separate out
nationalised industries. The published data often also lump
together productive assets such as machinery, with housing
which is essentially a durable consumer good. We give the
figures for the separate sectors leaving out dwellings. Finally,
in Table 3.4, we give the ratios of investment of various kinds
to gross domestic product.

Table 3.4 Investment (exclusive of dwellings) as a Proportion of Gross Domestic Product

	Private Sector	Government	Nationalised Industries	Total
1958	7.7	2.3	3.0	13.0
1959	7.7	2.4	3.2	13.3
1960	8.2	2.3	3.1	13.6
1961	8.7	2.3	3.3	14.3
1962	8.3	2.4	3.3	14.0
1963	7.8	2.4	3.4	13.6
1964	8.3	2.7	3.6	14.6
1965	8.4	2.6	3.6	14.6
1966	8.1	2.7	3.8	14.6
1967	7.8	3.0	4.2	15.0
1968	8.2	3.1	3.7	15.0
1969	8.7	3.2	3.0	14.9
1970	8.8	3.4	3.1	15.3
1971	8.7	3.2	3.1	15.0
1972	8.9	3.1	2.7	14.7
1973	9.3	3.8	2.6	15.7
1974	9.5	3.6	3.2	16.3
1975	8.9	3.1	3.5	15.5
1976	8.9	2.7	3.5	15.1
1977	9.6	2.0	3.1	14.7
1978	10.3	1.6	2.9	14.8
1979	10.6	1.6	2.7	14.9
1980	10.3	1.5	2.7	14.5
1981	9.5	1.2	2.7	13.4
1982	9.7	0.9	2.6	13.2

Starting with the figure for total investment excluding dwellings, it can be seen at once that this has a greater tendency to fluctuate every year than consumer spending does. That is in line with what elementary economic theory has to say, namely that investment is extremely sensitive to the climate of opinion concerning likely future profits and demand. Moreover, it reacts to changes in current demand conditions as exemplified by whether income is rising or falling.

Another comment worth making is that up to the

beginning of the seventies, for the most part the change in gross investment has been positive. Of the fourteen years from 1958 to 1971, in only one, 1962, did gross investment fall.

This leads on to the second point — more recently the average percentage change in investment has been negative almost as often as it has been positive. Altogether it rose by only about 4% in the period from 1972 to 1982.

We should pause here to note the significance of this. The level of net investment represents the increase in the capital stock. If investment is positive, the capital stock is rising. If investment is continuously rising at a constant rate, the capital stock will also be growing at that rate. A fall in the rate of rise of investment implies a fall in the rate of rise of the capital stock. The negative figures in Table 3.3, therefore, do not mean that investment was negative and that the capital stock was falling. Instead, their significance is that investment was lower in one year than it was in the previous one, and the capital stock was rising more slowly. (Even with the poor investment performance of 1974—80, the gross capital stock rose by about 3% per annum on average.)

We now proceed to look at the breakdown of the investment figures between the private sector, the government, and the nationalised industries. The first of these has always been more important than the combined figures for the other two. It has fluctuated from just over 50% of the total to more than 70%, but has not tended to exceed 60% until the last three years of the 1970s, and the first three years of the 1980s.

Private sector investment shows a pronounced cyclical character with boom years in 1961, 1964, 1968, 1973, 1977 and 1982. This is similar to but not precisely the same pattern as the economy as a whole. Concentrating as we are on annual figures it is impossible to establish the proposition that variations in private investment cause variations in general economic activity. A similar point applies to investment as a whole which sometimes seems to follow the changes in the economy, sometimes coincides with them and sometimes leads them. (It is worth reiterating here the remark made in the Introduction. More sophisticated technical methods and more detailed data, including quarterly statistics, would clarify this problem further, and disentangle how much investment is an independent cause of what happens in the economy and how much it transmits and augments other forces.)

A related theme concerns whether private sector and public sector investment move together or in opposite directions. It is easily seen that both nationalised industry investment and government investment have varied considerably from year to year. It is not the case that they have been a stable element of the economy. But have they been a stabilising element in the sense of varying inversely with private sector investment?

Once again, an unambiguous answer cannot be given. From the end of the 1950s until the end of the 1960s, public and private investment tended to move annually in opposite directions. A tendency for one to take a relatively larger share seemed to imply a tendency for the other to take a smaller share. This *could* be taken to mean that the public sector was a stabilising factor offsetting deficiencies in private sector investment when they occurred but also facilitating increases in that investment. An interpretation of that kind sees private sector investment as the independent destabilising force and public sector investment as the stabilising one. There is, however, an alternative view. It is that high public sector investment *crowds out* the private sector, and has to be held back to allow private sector investment to reach its appropriate level. This reverse direction of causation places the responsibility for fluctuations on the public sector.

Whatever conclusion is finally arrived at, it is apparent that the position changed in 1970. In six of the seven years from 1970 to 1976, public sector and private sector investment moved in the same direction. At the end of the decade yet another new situation emerged—several successive years of increases in private sector investment and decreases in public sector investment relative to gross domestic product. In the first two years of the 1980s all investment fell drastically. But in 1982 there was a significant recovery in private sector investment. This was associated with a recovery of output as a whole.

There are also some interesting points to be made about these trends. The material in Table 3.4 is plotted in Figure 3.3. It shows that the ratio of investment to gross domestic product has had no really strong upward trend since the beginning year or two of the 1960s. It has averaged about 15%, with 1963 and 1974 being extreme alternatives.

The position with respect to the private sector alone is rather different. Up to about 1970 there is no definite trend. But from then onwards the trend seems an upward one, most distinctly from the mid-1970s until 1979 when it is partly reversed.

Government investment (which, it should be recalled, includes such things as roads, schools etc.) presents a different picture. It is, of course, only a small fraction of national expenditure, but it does show an upward trend from 1958 to 1973. This is then followed by a much stronger downward movement so that, by 1982, it took its lowest share of gross domestic product in modern times.

There is one complication to do with the nationalised industries which must be stressed at once. Because particular firms and industries are nationalised, denationalised, renationalised, we are not comparing like with like every year. (As an example, the Post Office was a government department until 1966. It then became a nationalised industry, and some parts of that are currently being threatened with denationalisation, or what is now called privatisation.)

Overall, the ratio of nationalised industry investment to gross domestic product shows little trend. It has a very definite pattern though. It rises from 1958 to 1967, falls from 1967 to 1972, rises from 1972 to 1976, and then falls again. By 1982 it was below where it was at the beginning of the period. It is also interesting to note that the first and last phases show movement in the same direction as government investment. In the middle, the paths move in different directions. It is almost as if, at that time, the two forms of public sector investment were competing with each other, and that some of the rise in government investment was at the expense of the nationalised industries. Thus, for the six years 1969—74, nationalised industry investment was actually below that of the government sector.

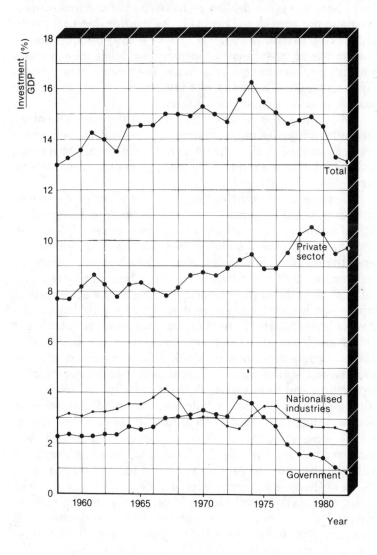

Figure 3.3

There is a great deal more to be said about investment. We have not considered explicitly its relationship to growth. This is discussed in Chapter 9. There is also the question of how much of investment is in manufacturing industry and how this is related to both growth and the balance of payments. That, together with the share of investment devoted to North Sea oil, is also discussed in Chapter 9.

We now go on to stock building. Although elementary accounts of macroeconomics tend to leave out the behaviour of stocks (or inventories as the Americans call them), no realistic account of UK economic experience is satisfactory without them.

Before examining their actual degree of variation, however, let us consider their general role in the economy. The production of services takes place at the same time as its consumption or demand. Of goods, some of them are made to order in the sense that demand is not met immediately it appears. Instead, the demand itself is the trigger for a production process, and will then be fulfilled some time later. This is true of all sorts of capital goods, at the one extreme, and for bespoke suits at the other. Having said that, most demand for goods is met when it shows itself, and this is possible because of the existence of stocks. Production adds to stocks, sales reduce stocks. In other words, stocks are a residual arising from the net effect of production and sales flows. A rise in production relative to sales in the economy as a whole leads to an accumulation of stocks. A rise in sales relative to production implies destocking.

Suppose sales start to rise unexpectedly. Stocks will fall, and if the new level of sales is expected to continue, the signal will be transmitted to producers to add to their output. This will be both to meet the new level of sales, and to restore stocks to an appropriate level. In addition, if the rise in sales is regarded as an indicator of further rises, production will increase more, and stocks will rise further. Thus, the response to a rise in demand and sales is a fluctuating path for stocks. They will fall, then rise, for a while above a new equilibrium level and then settle down to the new equilibrium.

A similar argument applies to a fall in sales. The result will be a rise in stocks as sales expectations are not met, followed by a fall and then a move to a new equilibrium.

Now, the point can be taken further. If, for example, sales are expected to fall in the future, even if they are not doing so now (or are expected to fall more than they are currently doing), producers, wholesalers, and retailers may anticipate this, and start to run down their stocks, by not reordering or placing new orders. Thus, production will fall, followed by income via the usual multiplier process. Equally, an expected rise in sales may be anticipated leading to production and a stock boom ahead of demand.

It is easy to see, therefore, both how stock building and destocking can cause economic fluctuations based on sales expectations and can transmit fluctuations caused by other forces. Nonetheless, stocks are a vital part of the functioning of the market economy which could hardly work if all production depended entirely on previously committed orders.

In Figure 3.4 we show how the *level* of stock building has fluctuated from year to year. This is given in constant prices. It is apparent that it changes so much from year to year that there is no point in plotting its percentage change. Between 1962 and 1964, for example, the rate of stock building tripled, while from 1974 to 1975 it went from +£2.8bn to −£2.9bn. What is also of interest is the enormous fall in stocks in 1980, 1981 and 1982. Some of this will have been a consequence of the depression in those years, and some a cause.

Since the wild fluctuations are expressed as levels in Figure 3.4, it might be thought that dividing them by gross domestic product would give a less exaggerated picture. This is true as Figure 3.5 demonstrates. Nonetheless, that figure still shows that stock building ranges from +2.2% of GDP to −1.4%. That will be a reflection of the behaviour of GDP itself, but as our theoretical comments indicate, will also be a cause of fluctuations in income and output.

As background it is worth mentioning for the umpteenth time the difference in behaviour of the series between the period up to 1973 and the period after that. In the earlier period the fluctuations, though large, were less than in the later period. In addition, some years of the later period show very significant destocking.

Of those years, 1975, 1980 and 1981 were ones in which national output fell. They were also years following a down-

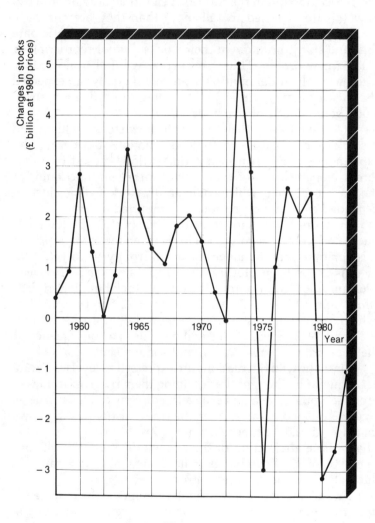

Figure 3.4

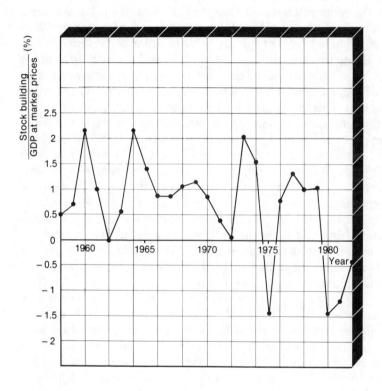

Figure 3.5

turn. This suggests the causal sequence was one of a fall in demand, leading to a fall in stock building, leading to a fall in output (and, perhaps, a further fall in demand etc.). A similar argument applies to 1962 and 1966–7 where the rate of stock building reached its minimum a year or so after the downturn in the economy began. In the 1961, 1965, and 1974 downturns, stock building was also falling compared with the previous year. There is left the slightly more peculiar behaviour of stock building towards the end of the 1960s and the beginning of the 1970s. It will be recalled that the economy went into a recession in 1969, from which it emerged less than fully in 1971. Output in that year expanded by less than was thought to be the economy's underlying growth rate, so that there was not really an outright boom. There was then a pause in 1972. Throughout the same period the ratio of stocks to GDP was falling. This suggests that a decision not to maintain stocks at their same ratio to GDP may have been a contributing factor to the behaviour of output. The coincidence of a fall in stocks in 1980 and 1981 with a fall in output makes it hard to distinguish cause from effect. At the very least, the reduction in stock accelerated the decline in output. What is interesting is that stocks went on falling in 1982 (albeit at a slower rate) even though output started to recover.

One last question is whether stocks anticipate or follow the upswing. In 1963, 1968, 1973, and 1976, the level of stock building rose compared with the previous year, and these were all years of upswing. In three of those years stocks also went on rising. In 1974, however, the level of stock building fell (although it remained positive), and GDP also fell. Moreover, in 1978 stock building fell compared with the previous year, although that was a boom year for output.

The conclusion that suggests itself is that a decision on the part of firms to add to their stocks can help an upswing to occur, and may have been one causal factor among others in helping some recessions to end. Similarly, a decision to cut the rate of adding to stocks may help to cause a downturn, as well as lead to the downturn continuing.

Apart from giving an overview of the behaviour of some of the components of national income, this chapter has also asked whether that behaviour is compatible with economic theory. On the whole it is — although we have left a great many problems unsolved. We have also seen in several cases the standard problem of applied economics, namely how hard it is to disentangle cause from effect. Both investment and stock building may have been causes of economic fluctuations, but it is likely that they have both been affected by them as well. Consumer spending has shown some stability, but the trend rise of the savings ratio and especially its increase in the 1970s is not easily explained in the sense of choosing one of the many possible causes. Lastly, public sector investment spending may have helped to stabilise the economy, but it is at least possible that it crowded out some private investment on occasion.

Questions

1. We have classified consumer goods according to whether they are durable or not. Elementary economic theory suggests that total consumer expenditure is determined by personal disposable income. What other variables might be important? Would they influence the purchase of durables and non-durables to the same degree?

2. It is said that there exists a black economy. In this, services are performed for cash payment, but receipts are not recorded for tax purposes. How would the black economy affect the statistics of national income and its components? Would a rise in the relative significance of the black economy influence the measurement of the propensity to consume?

3. It is sometimes stated that changes in consumption lag behind changes in income. Why might this be so?

4. How might consumption in the present be affected by:

    (a) an expectation that income will be lower in the future than had previously been anticipated;

    (b) an expectation that income will be more uncertain and variable in the future than had previously been anticipated?

5. What sort of economic variables would you expect to influence private sector investment? If investment is strongly influenced by expectations of future demand and profitability, is it essentially unpredictable?

6. Gross investment differs from net investment by the amount of capital used up during the period. Can you think of reasons why this depreciation (or capital consumption) would be difficult to measure?

7. If investment is expected to fluctuate, is that likely to influence whether, in fact, it does fluctuate?

8. What sort of costs are involved in holding stocks of goods? What policies might the government introduce if it wished to stabilise stocks?

9. Stocks exist to meet unexpected variations in demand. In the case of services, there can be no stocks. How might unexpected variations in demand be dealt with?

10. Would you expect production to be more stable in sectors in which stocks can be held than in service sectors?

4
Unemployment

Modern macroeconomics grew out of anxiety concerning unemployment in the 1930s. Neither economists nor politicians understood why unemployment occurred and persisted. Policy measures to deal with it lacked a theoretical underpinning, and government on occasion adopted policies which exacerbated the difficulties. It was felt to be a matter of urgency to solve the problem for its own sake, and also because it threatened our democratic way of life. The role of policy was to achieve 'full employment in a free society'. For the quarter century from 1945–70 it appeared that success was attained and easily so.

In the 1970s unemployment rose drastically, as did inflation. In addition, for the first time opinion polls showed that the public at large were more worried about price rises than the fact that more and more people were losing their jobs. But by the end of the 1970s — although, as we shall see, the inflation problem was not solved — unemployment took over again as the key issue exercising everybody's mind.

The simplest approach to the subject goes as follows:

(a) demand fluctuates
(b) production fluctuates
(c) employment fluctuates
(d) unemployment fluctuates

This is the so-called Keynesian view of the matter. (To be added to it is the proposition that demand has a chronic tendency to be below full employment levels, giving rise to chronic unemployment.) In interpreting it, a vital point to bear in mind is that 'demand' means 'real demand', i.e. nominal demand relative to the price level. A rise in money expenditure may not cause more sales or more production if it is accompanied by an actual or expected rise in prices.

In addition to short-term fluctuations in employment and unemployment, there are long-term tendencies to be taken into account as well. There are demographic and social factors such as size of population, and attitudes of married women to work to be considered. The long-run supply of labour will be influenced by education and training facilities. On more narrowly economic grounds, the nature of the technology will influence the demand for labour and capital. How much employment corresponds to full employment will then depend on the real wage that workers demand, and the ratio of the cost of labour to the cost of machines. (Turning the matter on its head, if technology and capital investment are labour saving, the same number of men can only be employed if they receive a real wage lower than would otherwise be the case.)

Reference may also be made to the kind of unemployment which depends on the relationship between social security benefits and wages net of tax, the so-called replacement ratio. An unemployed person may seek a job less vigorously if the loss of income involved in not having one is less significant. (Relevant too may be the degree of pressure brought on the unemployed by the people operating the social security system.)

This second longer-run view of the matter is sometimes referred to as classical, and in this form is not necessarily incompatible with the Keynesian approach to the problem. Thus, unemployment may rise because aggregate demand falls, and may stay high because demand fails to rise again. Superimposed on that may be even more unemployment due to technical and institutional change, and failure of relative prices to adjust appropriately.

We may summarise by saying that unemployment may exist because employers do not wish to take on additional workers, or because workers do not wish to accept jobs currently being offered. The former may be for two reasons: (a) lack of demand for the goods and services the workers produce; (b) excess real wage demands, making it unprofitable to produce more output and take on extra workers. The latter may also occur for two reasons: (a) the pay and conditions are worse than the minimum acceptable to potential employees; (b) the pay and conditions are worse than the worker expects to find elsewhere if he searches a bit more.

With that general background let us look more precisely at the actual figures. In doing so, it is important to distinguish the concept of unemployment as it is used by economists from the way unemployment is actually measured by the government's statisticians. This is especially so because recently the method of measurement has been changed in rather a significant manner.

Typically in economics a person is regarded as involuntarily unemployed if he is able and willing to work in return for rewards similar to those which existing workers are already getting. The point holds *a fortiori* if he is willing to work for less. Someone who is capable of working but is only available on superior terms, may be unemployed but is said to be voluntarily so. It should be added that in practice it is extremely difficult to make the distinction between voluntary and involuntary unemployment.

Until 1982 the measurement of the number of people unemployed consisted of those people who were available for work and who were registered as such. It did not, therefore, include all those who previously were employed. In the UK there are a number of workers who are not eligible for unemployment and related benefits. Although they may have lost their jobs, they are not required to join the register, and may, therefore, choose not to do so. The reason may be that they are using other methods to seek work, or may, indeed, feel discouraged from doing so altogether in the existing circumstances. This group comprises chiefly married women. A second notable group of the formerly employed are men who retire on losing their jobs, but who would have carried on longer in employment if they had not been fired. Although they do not register, some of these too might return to work in more propitious circumstances.

In 1982 a new method of measuring unemployment was introduced. Essentially, the unemployed were deemed to consist of those people who had lost their jobs and now collected social security. A number of other minor adjustments were made, and the overall effect was to simplify the method of estimation, but also to reduce the numbers so estimated.

The official definition of the unemployed is now 'people

claiming benefit (that is, unemployment benefit, supplementary benefits or national insurance credits) at Unemployment
Benefit Offices on the day of the monthly count, who on that
day were unemployed and able and willing to do any suitable
work. (Students claiming benefit during a vacation and who
intend to return to full-time education are excluded.)'

For this kind of reason the change in employment is not
the same as the negative of the change in unemployment. In
addition, of course, some people enter the unemployed state
directly, that is with not having been previously employed.
The obvious members of this category are school leavers. It
follows that, if employment falls (say) by 100,000, unemployment may rise by a figure different from this. Ignoring school
leavers, unemployment may rise by less than 100,000. Similarly,
if employment rises by 100,000, unemployment may fall by
less than that. Until recently, the ratio of the change in
unemployment to employment was about 1 to 2. Now the ratio
is nearer to 2 to 3.

A person who registers as unemployed essentially
announces his availability on existing terms and conditions of
employment, relative to his capability, qualifications, and
experience. The figures would not include an unskilled worker
who claimed to be available as a brain surgeon. They do,
however, include people who might not be available for work
on terms and in conditions noticeably worse than those currently received by the comparable employed. This is so even
though on general macroeconomic grounds an extension of
employment might require a relative deterioration in pay and
other benefits.

Of course, workers differ in the likelihood of their obtaining jobs. Some, even in depressed conditions, can expect to be
back in work with a delay of a few months at most. Others
will be most unlikely to obtain a job rapidly even in boom
conditions. Nonetheless, this latter group is largely made up
of workers who were in jobs. Moreover, on past experience,
many of those with poor prospects did obtain jobs when an
economic upturn occurred. Very few of the registered
unemployed are strictly unemployable, especially in general
conditions of labour market buoyancy.

The figure for total unemployed is what economists call a

stock. In simplest terms, the number of unemployed rises if the *flow* of those joining the stock exceeds the flow of those leaving it. The stock of unemployed is akin to a reservoir, the level of which rises or falls depending on whether the rate of water flowing in exceeds that of water flowing out.

It follows that unemployment is very much a dynamic phenomenon. To say that adult unemployment in 1983 was approximately 3.0m. does not mean that 3.0m. people were out of jobs for the whole of 1983. Of course some were (and some were out of jobs for even longer); but the average comprises many more people out of work for rather shorter periods of time. This means that if, for example, the average period of unemployment were six months, and nobody had more than one spell of unemployment in a year, about five million people experienced unemployment in 1981. Actually, some people do have multiple spells of unemployment and are even what may be called unemployment prone. Nonetheless, it remains true that in 1983 something between 5 and 6 million workers did get on the register. (There were also some workers who lost their jobs and got new jobs all within a month, and never got into the statistics at all.)

The stock of unemployed is equal to the rate at which workers join the register times the average time they spend there before getting a job. If, for example, 400,000 workers a month join the register and each stays there for six months, the stock of unemployed would equal 2.4m.

As an arithmetic example suppose we start from scratch with zero unemployed.

Month	Unemployed joining the register	Leaving the register	Total unemployed
1	400,000	0	400,000
2	400,000	0	800,000
3	400,000	0	1,200,000
4	400,000	0	1,600,000
5	400,000	0	2,000,000
6	400,000	0	2,400,000
7	400,000	400,000	2,400,000
8	400,000	400,000	2,400,000

After the sixth month the numbers flowing off the register into jobs exactly equals the new people on the register. Therefore, the stock of unemployed reaches a stable equilibrium value.

It is now easy to see that the total unemployed column will rise if (a) the average period of unemployment rises, or (b) if the rate of flow onto the register rises. It is simple to rework the example with the average period of unemployment at 7 months. Total unemployment would then increase to 2.8m. Similarly, if the flow in rose to 467,000 total unemployment would again increase to 2.8m. Notice that, if the flow did rise to 467,000, it would take six months for the stock to rise to its new equilibrium level.

In the period we are examining both these phenomena have occurred, namely that the flows on to the register have risen and the average period has also gone up. The two together can cause a dramatic rise in the numbers of unemployed as the experience of 1980—3 demonstrates. Suppose the typical flow on to the register is 250,000 per month and the average period spent on the register were 6 months, total unemployment would be 1.5m. A rise of a flow on to the register to 375,000 and an increase of the average period to 8 months would cause the stock of unemployed to reach 3m., i.e. double.

The actual time path has, not surprisingly, been more complicated than this. In Table 4.1 we give some figures for flows into and out of unemployment between 1979 and 1983. Deducting one from another, the net increase in the size of the pool is obtained. It is easy to see how this net increase has risen. If the typical rate of increase per month is taken to be

Table 4.1 Unemployment Flows for Great Britain (3-month averages)

	Flows On (+) ('000)	Flows Off (−) ('000)	Difference ('000)
April 1979	270	271	−1
April 1980	303	267	36
April 1981	343	277	66
April 1982	333	324	9
April 1983	306	330	−24

that for (say) April 1981, this implies an annual addition to the stock of 800,000 people. Since then the rate of increase has slackened, and by the middle of 1983 showed signs of becoming zero. Concerning the actual path of unemployment, there has been a large increase in the long-term unemployed. At the beginning of 1980, the number of people unemployed for a year or more was about 340,000. This had risen to about 440,000 by the beginning of 1981 and 780,000 by the end of that year. By the middle of 1983 the long-term unemployed numbered 1.1 million. In addition, the fraction of young people (that is, 25-year olds and less) in that category had risen from 15% of the total to 30%.

Let us now examine the unemployment figures in more detail. (The figures leave out transitory factors due to the seasons, for example, and are for adults, wholly unemployed. The so-called 'headline' unemployment figures quoted in newspapers exceed these figures when, for example, school leavers are added.) They are tabulated as a percentage in Table 4.2 and then shown in Figure 4.1. There are several points about that figure that stand out. Consider the following:

(i)   During the 1950s and 1960s unemployment fluctuated a little, but remained typically in the range 1.3% to 2.3%.
(ii) At the end of the 1960s there was an upward rise in unemployment, which was not reversed.
(iii) There were subsequently three further significant rises in unemployment, all of which were only partially reversed. In absolute and percentage terms, the biggest of these occurred between 1980 and 1981/82.

The result has been a continuously rising trend of unemployment. It seems that there have been a series of cyclical fluctuations giving rise on each occasion to new peaks of unemployment, which are not wholly offset when the economy starts to boom again. (As a matter of historical record, it should also be borne in mind that these peaks of unemployment correspond to contractionary movements in the economy deliberately imposed by the governments of the time. They were connected with a desire to deal with problems of the balance of payments and inflation. While their cumulative effect has been adverse, it is not likely that the respective

Chancellors of the Exchequer precisely expected the outcomes that occurred or actually desired them.)

Although the most noticeable increases in unemployment occur from 1967 onwards, it may be remarked that an upward trend, albeit a slight one, starts earlier. An examination of the unemployment peaks from 1959 onwards indicates that each one was above its predecessor. It is reasonable to suggest, therefore, that, while the rise in chronic unemployment may be attributable to a number of powerful forces coming into play at the end of the 1970s, there was some difficulty in maintaining full employment before that.

Table 4.2 Unemployment as a Percentage of the Total Work Force for the UK

1959	2.1
1960	1.7
1961	1.5
1962	2.0
1963	2.3
1964	1.7
1965	1.4
1966	1.5
1967	2.3
1968	2.5
1969	2.4
1970	2.6
1971	3.4
1972	3.7
1973	2.6
1974	2.6
1975	3.9
1976	5.3
1977	5.8
1978	5.7
1979	5.3
1980	6.8
1981	10.5
1982	12.2
1983	12.7

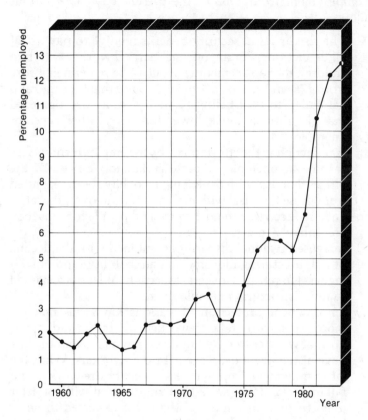

Figure 4.1

Why then has unemployment risen? Let us start with the so-called structural explanations. There are a number of these which economists have examined and assessed. Together they may account for perhaps 500,000 of the 2.5—3.0m. increase in unemployment from 1962 to the present day. They are as follows:

(i)   The rise in social security benefits relative to pay net of all deductions. For an average married worker with two children the replacement ratio as we have defined it rose from 47% in 1963 to 76% in 1971. Since that time the ratio has fallen to well below 70%. It should also be noted that the ratio is much lower for many other types of unemployed.

(ii)   A reduction in the efforts made by the employment service to make an unemployed person take a job. Since 1973 the offices that deal with benefit payment have been separated from those that deal with placement. Moreover, the latter have reduced their tendency to send people for jobs they are unlikely to get.

(iii)   Increased regional disparities combined with the decline of manufacturing industry and an inability (and unwillingness) to retrain workers, especially older ones, has led to more structural unemployment.

(iv)   Employment protection of various kinds has made it more expensive to take on workers (that is, in addition to normal wage costs). Redundancy payments and the like have also made it dearer to get rid of workers. While the latter may make employers less likely to fire workers if a fall in demand is regarded as temporary, it will not deter them from such a move if the fall is expected to be of longer duration. After that it will be a major deterrent to taking them on again.

All of these considerations are of possible importance — the problem is to attach a numerical weight to them. Economists are not in agreement on this, especially as there are many theoretical difficulties in distinguishing structural causes of unemployment from sheer lack of demand. Nonetheless, in the mid-1960s it would have been said that at full employment about 400,000 to 500,000 of the labour force would have been out of work and seeking a job, i.e. something between 1.5% and 2.5% of the labour force. Nowadays, the range of variations of informed opinion is between 750,000 and 1,250,000, i.e. between 4% and 5% of the labour force. (Of course, there are also economists and others with more extreme views.) In other words, structural factors have at least doubled the sustainable level of unemployment. Even that, however, leaves between 1.75m. and 2.25m. unemployed for more general macroeconomic reasons.

These, as we have remarked, are of two sorts and are again extremely hard to disentangle. On the one hand, real demand for goods and services is too low. On the other hand, real wages are too high, making it unprofitable to meet an increase in demand.

Concerning the latter, there are two points to be made. One is that the rise in the price of oil demanded by OPEC in 1973 lowered the real income available to British workers. At the same time, capital equipment and productive processes which used a lot of energy became obsolete, and unprofitable to use. The two together may have reduced the demand for labour at any given real wage. In addition, the growth potential of the economy probably fell, that reduction being reinforced by the associated stagnation. It follows that not only was there a fall in the level of full employment real wages, but also a fall in their rate of growth. If at the same time workers pressed for higher real wages still, the so-called classical factors would have been intensified. In this connection, it must be noted that real wages in the 1970s did rise relative to productivity.

Light may also be thrown on this problem by placing it in an international context. The profitability of exports depends on the revenue received from foreign purchasers relative to the costs incurred largely at home. If the external value of sterling is high, this will lower the foreign demand for our goods and put pressure on manufacturers to cut their sterling price. Suppose at the same time money wages are rising even faster. Profits will then be squeezed, making marginal production unprofitable. This means that if domestic demand did rise, it might not be profitable for home producers to supply it. The demand would then spill over into imports, creating employment abroad but not in the UK. The rise in the money wage relative to the external value of sterling was an important cause of the rise in unemployment in Britain. More generally, there was a new trend of world inflation attributable, to a great extent, to a rise in the price of oil at the end of the 1970s. Governments met this by contracting their economies, producing a world depression and adding to unemployment.

The conclusion to be drawn from this is that the path back to full employment (whatever that is) is a difficult and slow one. It is apparent that a full employment policy involves an expansion of real demand, that is demand in money terms must increase relative to prices. If, however, more workers are to be taken on, it must be profitable to do so. Real wages must not, therefore, rise relative to productivity, nor must the expansion of demand be expected to be temporary. Separate from that there must be structural changes in the economy connected with industrial retraining, increased labour flexibility and mobility, and the reversal of deindustrialisation. (More of all this is discussed in Chapter 9 on growth.)

Questions

1.   How might 'labour saving' be defined? Is it the same thing as labour being more productive?

2.   A cut in income tax raises wages net of taxes. Will this necessarily cause more unemployed workers to take the sorts of jobs offered to them?

3.   We have noted that the ratio of the change in unemployment to the change in employment has risen in recent years. Why might this have occurred? What information would you require to test whether you are right?

4.   Some unemployed people apply for jobs and are rejected on the grounds that they are 'over qualified' for them. Why might this be so?

5.   Why might some people be more prone to unemployment than others? Would you expect this to depend on personality factors, or on more economic characteristics?

6.   With our discussion of structural factors (including so-
     called frictional ones) as a background, how would you
     define 'full employment'? Is it correct to define this concept
     solely in economic terms?

7.   Suppose that for some people the level of benefits out of
     work compared with net income in work was so high
     that they tended to reject the jobs that were available.
     Does this necessarily raise the level of unemployment?
     Consider the possibility that it merely means that other
     people can more easily get these jobs.

5
Inflation

The main subject of this chapter is UK inflation since the 1960s. Its broader theme is that of inflation in general, including inflation elsewhere in the world. In considering the behaviour of prices, it is necessary also to pay attention to wages, unemployment, and the balance of payments. These are discussed mainly in other chapters and only limited reference is made to them here. Instead we shall concentrate on the basic facts, leaving some of the theorising until later.

The economy of the United Kingdom is inflation prone. In Chapter 2, the price index we examined was the so-called gross domestic product deflator. An examination of that shows that for every year since 1959, for example, the average level of prices has risen compared with the preceding year. (A similar conclusion follows from the retail price index and other indices of final prices.) The inflation rate has followed a cyclical pattern, although not one of precisely constant frequency. Up to the end of the 1960s there tended to be two or three years of rising inflation rates followed by two or three years of falling rates. The average inflation rate from 1959 to 1969 was about 3.5% per annum, and, while no annual figures were negative, none were in double figures. The 'frequency distribution' of the inflation rate in this period is shown in Table 5.1. This tells us that in two years the inflation rate was 1—2% per annum, in another two years it was 2—3%, and so on.

Since 1969, the annual inflation rate has increased significantly, and has been above the average for the period 1948—68 in every year. Moreover, the annual rate was in

Table 5.1 The Frequency Distribution of the Inflation Rate for
1959—69

Inflation Rate	Frequency (number of years)
0—1%	0
1—2%	2
2—3%	2
3—4%	3
4—5%	2
> 5%	2

double figures from 1974 to 1981. In 1982 it fell to single
figures. It fell further in 1983, but at about 5% still exceeded
the average for the 1960s. Another interesting characteristic of
the more recent period is that for the first time the inflation
rate rose in four successive years, from 1968—71. Indeed, in
the eight years 1968—75 there were six accelerations and only
two decelerations—1972 and '73. Since the pause then was
only a comparatively modest one, we actually experienced a
steady climb in the inflation rate starting in 1968 and not really
being reversed until 1976. There was a further acceleration of
the inflation rate between 1978 and 1980, which has been
subsequently reversed.

Let us now examine the figures for the change in prices as
they are set out in Table 5.2 and Figure 5.1. (Concentrate on
the first column of Table 5.2, the percentage change in the
gross domestic product deflator. This refers to the average
change of the prices of all the final goods and services sold in
the economy.) What is remarkable about the figure is that
there is an upward trend in inflation which seems to start
either in 1959 or 1962, depending on whether it is the trough or
peak that is focused on. Concentrating just on the 1960s, the
trend is small, but over the whole period it is quite distinctive.
Moreover it does look as if there is some kind of ratchet at
work in that each peak (or trough) is higher than the preceding
one. This suggests that, if we have entered a new era of inflation, the point of departure, although not its only cause, goes
back a long way in time.

Table 5.2 Annual Percentage Changes in Prices

	GDP Deflator	Consumer Expenditure Deflator	Government Expenditure Deflator
1960	1.7	1.1	3.8
1961	3.4	3.0	3.7
1962	3.8	4.0	7.1
1963	2.1	1.4	0.0
1964	3.6	3.8	6.7
1965	5.4	4.5	6.3
1966	4.2	4.3	5.9
1967	3.1	2.5	5.6
1968	4.3	4.9	5.3
1969	5.4	5.4	5.0
1970	7.1	5.9	14.3
1971	9.2	8.7	8.3
1972	8.4	6.4	11.5
1973	7.2	8.4	6.9
1974	14.8	17.2	22.6
1975	27.1	23.6	31.6
1976	14.9	15.9	16.0
1977	13.9	14.9	10.3
1978	11.0	8.8	10.9
1979	14.5	13.5	14.0
1980	19.8	16.4	23.5
1981	11.6	11.1	13.0
1982	7.2	8.4	8.8

Nonetheless, it is not until the late 1960s that something really unusual stands out. Viewed from today's standpoint it might be possible to say that by 1965 concern ought to have been expressed about a rising inflation trend. If that is thought too harsh a judgment, because the inflation rate in that year was not very much above the peak of 1961–2 (and was actually below the peak of 1956), the alarm bells should have been ringing in 1967. In that year the inflation rate at the trough was above that at the previous three troughs. More generally, as we have already remarked, what is noteworthy is the increase in the inflation rate from 1967 onwards. By 1970 it was higher than at any time for sixteen years, and had risen for the third

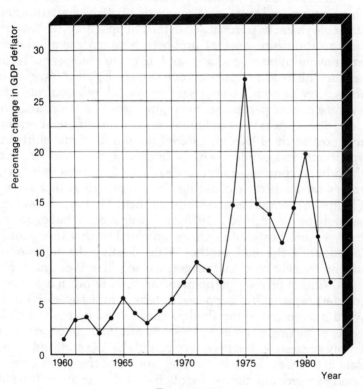

Figure 5.1

year in succession. What this means is that, as far as the UK is concerned, the oil price rise was not the original cause of the new inflation (whatever that turns out to be), but a major shock superimposed on an already deteriorating situation.

Sticking to our elementary methods, let us now recall that there is supposed to be some connection between inflation and unemployment as summarised in the Phillips curve. This statistical relationship was first proposed between wage inflation and unemployment, and was not original to Phillips, but let us set such historical niceties on one side. In Figure 5.2 we show the scatter of points comprising an annual inflation rate and average annual percentage unemployment. To the naked eye there does appear to be a glimmering of an inverse relationship for most of the 1960s. In 1968—9 the inflation rate shifts up apparently independently of the unemployment position, and the process continues during the earlier 1970s. Although this is rather far-fetched, it could just be hypothesised that a new Phillips curve was being established then. That too, however, seems to be overturned in 1975, and again it could be suggested that yet another Phillips curve appeared at that time which lasted until the end of the 1970s. Lastly, the inflation—unemployment combination gets worse still in 1980 and 1981.

Without pressing the point too hard, therefore, it is possible to interpret what has happened in terms of the successive outward movement of the Phillips curve, the key pushes, as it were, occurring in 1968—9, 1974—5, and 1980. Of course, this is only suggestive. It is necessary to add that the partition of the data in this way, let alone the suggestion that the points correspond to a series of curves, hardly meet the rigorous criteria of statistical analysis. Nonetheless, approaching the subject in historical terms and using only the simplest of methods does enable us to focus on what might be certain important questions. In particular, the identification of 1968—9, 1974—5, and 1980—1 as years worthy of closer consideration might lead to the beginnings of an answer to the causes of rising inflation and unemployment. At the very least we might be aided in any attempt to reject some of the available explanations.

Before mentioning some of these there are some additional points concerning the data in Table 5.2. We have concentrated so far on the first of these, which is strictly speaking an index

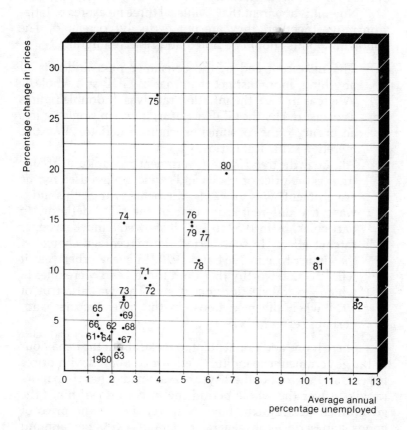

Figure 5.2

of the prices of goods and services sold in the economy, net of indirect taxes and subsidies. The second column refers to consumer goods only, and is at market prices. The third column refers to the goods and services purchased by the government.

Now, it is apparent that, while all three measures of inflation move together, they are not perfectly correlated. The following points should be noted and reflected upon:

(a)   The upward trend in the consumer price index is, if anything, more distinct than that of GDP as a whole.

(b)   Whereas in 1978 the inflation rate was in double figures as measured by the GDP deflator, it was in single figures according to the consumer expenditure deflator. Was this merely a statistical curiosity?

(c)   Although the trend in the government expenditure deflator (that is the price of goods and services purchased by the government) was upwards, the behaviour of this index was very different from that of the GDP deflator. In particular, from 1959 to 1973 it showed a much stronger ratchet effect. In that period the percentage change in that index rose in 1964 and 1970. In every other year it fell. It is noteworthy that both those years were ones in which general elections occurred. (This was also true of 1974 when the next boost in the index occurs, and, perhaps, even in 1979.)

There is one additional point to make about the behaviour of the government expenditure deflator compared with prices in general. In 16 out of the 23 years examined, it has risen more rapidly. Over the whole period the prices of the things the government has bought have risen relative to the price of goods and services in general by about 1.5% per annum. There are several possible explanations of this phenomenon, which is called the *relative price effect*:

(a)   The public sector is labour intensive compared with the economy as a whole. Since money wages have a general tendency to rise compared with prices (that is real wages have a tendency to grow), a labour intensive service finds its relative costs rising.

(b)   The public sector has a tendency on occasion to pay excessive wages for some services.

(c)   The way public sector output is measured tends to under-
       estimate gains in productivity there. This would under-
       estimate the true scale of the services provided and
       overestimate their costs (which we defined as equal to
       expenditure divided by scale of service).

Reverting to our general theme, explanations of inflation
may be clarified as follows:

(a)   whether they refer to global causes or specifically UK
       causes,
(b)   whether they refer to demand factors or supply factors,
(c)   whether they see the problem arising from the public
       sector or the private sector.

Economists also differ as to whether they emphasise a
single cause (e.g. too fast a growth of the money supply, or
excessive trade union militancy) or many causes (excessive
growth of the money supply *and* trade union militancy *and*
OPEC and so on). The account presented here is certainly
multi-causal.

Typical external explanations presented are:

(a)   The inflationary financing of the Vietnam War in 1965—6
       by the Americans; this led to an increase in the world
       money supply, world liquidity, and global excess demand
       for basic commodities.
(b)   A European boom at the end of the 1960s connected, in
       particular, with possibly excessive expansion of the W.
       German economy.
(c)   Labour unrest especially in Paris in 1968, signalling an
       increased degree of aggressive wage push generally in
       1969.
(d)   The OPEC oil price explosions of 1973 and 1979.

Although these forces are relevant to the UK, they do not
tell the whole story. Nearly all countries have experienced an
upward drift in inflation since 1959 but they differ with respect
to magnitude and timing of the higher inflation rates. Thus, to
answer the question: 'Why did UK inflation rise in the 1960s
and 1970s?' it is not enough to give the answer, 'because world
inflation did'.

In Table 5.3 we give some comparison of European infla-

Table 5.3 Inflation Percentage Per Annum, European Countries

	1950—60	1961—72	1973—83
Austria	3.3	3.5	6.0
Belgium	1.5	3.5	8.2
France	5.2	4.4	11.4
W. Germany	1.9	3.0	4.8
Italy	2.6	3.9	17.1
Netherlands	2.6	4.8	6.6
Norway	3.5	4.7	9.8
Sweden	3.6	4.4	10.2
UK	3.3	4.6	13.7

tion rates. In the 1950s UK inflation was about average. In the 1960s it rose a little above average. In the 1970s it was well above average. (It is worth remarking that by the end of 1983, UK inflation was 0.5% below the average for the advanced industrialised world.)

One domestic explanation of inflation that is offered concerns the membership of trade unions. A second is that the full employment position of the economy has deteriorated, i.e. the so-called natural rate of unemployment has gone up. If the latter proposition were true, governments attempting to run the economy at what was once a feasible unemployment rate will now find it overheating.

On trade unions, as a fraction of total employees, membership was remarkably steady in the first period we are examining, being at about 43% from the early 1960s onwards. To the extent, therefore, that the upward creep in economic difficulties started in this period, a greater tendency to have joined trade unions cannot have been the cause. It is noteworthy, however, that trade union membership jumped significantly in 1970 to 48% of total employees. It is necessary to add that this was also the first year that the average percentage increase in earnings went into double figures, a state of affairs which persisted for more than a decade.

Some economists treat the growth of trade union membership at its face value, that is as an indicator of greater militancy and a tendency to press for higher wages, coupled with greater strength to resist reductions in wage increases. It follows that, to the extent that the labour market is at all important, greater slack must be introduced there to achieve the same rate of wage inflation. In other words, increased unionisation moves the Phillips curve to the right. Now, other economists, observing the same increase in wage inflation, assert that the natural rate of unemployment has risen, i.e. the Phillips curve has moved to the right. Moreover, they accept that this can be the result of increased unionisation and the greater militancy of workers. It appears, therefore that, despite the theoretical arguments that rage, the two statements, 'higher inflation is due to greater wage push', and 'higher inflation is due to an increase in the natural rate of unemployment', can and probably do amount to the same thing, despite the monetarist nature of the latter and the anti-monetarist nature of the former.

More generally, on the natural rate of unemployment (i.e. the amount of unemployment that exists at full employment), we did see in Chapter 4 that it may have risen because of structural factors. We shall also see in Chapter 9 that the underlying rate of growth of the economy may have fallen in the mid-1970s compared with earlier periods. It follows that inflation (and stagflation, i.e. inflation with high unemployment and low growth) can result both because the government attempts to achieve an impossible full employment target and unions try to gain impossibly high real wages. We saw this above all in 1974–5 and after, when trades unions refused to accept that a transfer of real resources to OPEC implied an inevitable decline in their members' real incomes.

But that is only part of the story. It is also the case that there was excessive expansion of the economy in the so-called Barber boom of 1972–3, and associated with that was too great a monetary expansion. Furthermore sterling was allowed to float freely, and, insofar as it was tending to fall, it raised the price of our imports.

It is extremely important to place the so-called Barber boom in perspective. The rate of price inflation had been rising steadily from 1967 to 1971. Indeed, 1972 was a year of lower inflation compared with its immediate predecessor. It is also true that the money supply had been accelerating since 1972 and wages since 1968. Mr. Barber can be criticised for not damping down an inflation that was there and probably getting worse, rather than for adding to it, but it is not fair to suggest that he was the originator of the inflation in the first place. His experiment was dangerous, but at the time was not necessarily foolhardy, especially if it is accepted that the oil price explosion could not have been forecast.

Whatever view is taken of that, however, the behaviour of unemployment must not be ignored in this period. The unemployment percentage rose significantly in 1967, stayed at its new higher level for four years, and then jumped again in 1971 and 1972. Moreover, despite the strength of the Barber expansion which did cause employment to rise and unemployment to fall, the latter did not get back to its level of the 1950s and 1960s. It is hard to reject the view on this evidence that the new behaviour of the inflation rate is connected with new behaviour of the unemployment percentage. In other words, the arguments of earlier paragraphs must not be ignored.

Going back again to OPEC, it is apparent that the oil price increase in 1973 did raise inflation rates, in that fiscal and monetary policy were adjusted to allow the domestic price level to rise while not causing employment to fall too rapidly. Money wage increases continued to rise in 1974 and 1975, partly because workers refused to accept the new state of affairs, and indeed were still intent on recouping even earlier losses of real income.

It has been argued that, if tighter fiscal and monetary disciplines had been imposed at that time, the inflation rate would not have risen and equally the increase in unemployment would have been avoided. This view is based on a speed and degree of moderation of wage demands which has no basis on past experience in the UK. Much more likely would have been a faster rise in unemployment with only a small reduction in the inflation rate. Certainly, as more recent experience has shown, the swing round is to be measured in years and not months, and even now after much higher rates of unemployment than were contemplated either by Labour or Tory governments in 1970–4, inflation expectations are far from having been eradicated. (Examine Figure 5.2, for example, to note the extent of the rise in unemployment that accompanies the decline in inflation.)

In this connection, it is important not to ignore the political dimension. The circumstances in which Mr. Heath's government fell and a Labour government without an overall majority was elected in February 1974, do not appear in the economic time series that have been examined. Thus, while in retrospect it could be argued, probably correctly, that technically the macroeconomic posture in 1974 and 1975 should have been more restrictive in every way, such a policy of fiscal, monetary, and incomes constraints was by no means feasible in the circumstances. It will be recalled, for example, that as part of its incomes policy the Conservative government had included an index-linked element in wage changes to preserve their real value. Once the price of oil was raised, this was a promise which could not be met, unless unemployment were allowed to rise drastically, and perhaps not even then. The incoming Labour government should simply have gone back on the promise, on narrowly economic grounds but, in the circumstances, they can hardly be blamed for not doing so. A similar point could be made about the extent to which they increased transfer payments especially to old people as part of the social contract.

The culmination of all this was the very rapid rise of prices in 1974 and 1975, the causes of which were many and not one, namely too easy a fiscal stance, too rapid a rise in wages, the oil price rise and the fall in the exchange rate. All these interacted, and it is wrong to regard any as a first cause, although in this case the exchange rate should be regarded as part of the process of feedback rather than an initiating element in its own right.

Altogether, the experience of the mid-1970s and early 1980s serves mostly to reinforce what has gone before. This reinforcement is not trivial, however, for it serves to dispel the view that what had gone before was transitory. Higher inflation rates have taken longer to be brought under control than some economists had anticipated. Even now they have not gone away, and events from 1979–81 show how easily an improving trend can be reversed. The two key events to note are the second OPEC price explosion at the end of the decade which affected the whole world, and the wage explosion in 1979–80 which was peculiar to the UK. More seriously, unemployment has not yet been brought under control, and the outlook remains poor. In other words, stagflation has turned out not to be temporary, and is, therefore, a problem or class of problems as much for the economic historian as the theorist. Thus, any attempt to teach the subject must become involved with the interaction of price setting and quantity adjustment, that is, the agenda of the Phillips curve comprising wage and price change, on the one hand, and the level and rate of change of unemployment on the other. The fact that we no longer have a simple, stable Phillips curve does not mean that the class of problems which that curve illustrated has gone away.

There is one other aspect of inflation experience since 1975 that is worth emphasising. It is the role of incomes policy. Broadly speaking, the latest evidence on incomes policy is that, when it is on, the rate of increase in wages and prices slows down, but when it is off these variables return to the levels warranted by other economic forces. This result is often interpreted as being against incomes policy, but that is surely mistaken. The correct interpretation, especially of the 1970s experience, is, firstly, that incomes policy and monetary and fiscal policy must be complementary. If, for example, the fiscal and monetary stance of the government is such that the labour market is extremely buoyant, and it is widely believed that any wage settlement will be validated, it is impossible that incomes policy can be successful. Instead, it will be like the social contract of 1974–5, highly inflationary. Secondly, if incomes policy does succeed, in association with other policies, in restraining wage pressure, unless it is on for a very long time and associated with other institutional and structural changes, it is unlikely to change the underlying way the labour market works. Those economists who viewed it in educative terms, and believed that after a while a successful incomes policy could be abandoned with no ill effects, have probably been mistaken. Thirdly, therefore, what incomes policy does is to facilitate the use of other instruments, enabling the transition costs of anti-inflation policies to be reduced somewhat. It announces the extent to which the government will be willing to validate wage increases, and also provides some assurance about the maintenance of relativities at least in other than the very short term.

The Heath and Healey incomes policies both provided

valuable experience. They showed that no policy can provide a real income guarantee in excess of what is feasible. This was true both of the net transfer to OPEC and of the desire to increase social security payments. Even with the UK economy growing at its earlier maximum rate of 3% per annum, some of the burden of these transfers would have had to fall on wage earners. With a lower growth rate, they implied that real wages net of tax could hardly rise at all for a while.

Apart from that it is always true that incomes policy is subject to destructive forces. One is the standard one that, if all workers show restraint, it pays any group of workers to break ranks in order to maximise their own returns. Since every group can work this out logically, all are poised to destroy the system. This suggests that incomes policy is essentially unstable. If next it is noted that, when the policy breaks down, all will eventually lose, it might then be argued that this will act as a stabilising factor. The conclusion to be drawn is that collapse is not inevitable, but that maintaining the policy will always be hard work. The typical policy will fail in some years, especially when it is borne in mind that the sanctions which a government is likely to use will not affect all workers equally. This is especially true of unemployment which, in a context of strict monetary and fiscal control, does not fall wholly or even mainly on those who exert the strongest wage push. It should also not be forgotten that in a two-party system it is always tempting for the opposition to promise easier times and the end of restraint.

Paradoxically, therefore, one key lesson to be learned from the 1970s is the importance of the political element in economic policy. It may well be that Mr. Heath was getting policy technically correct in 1973—4, but the electorate did not give him a chance to demonstrate that. It is certain that, until the rather too expansionary Budget of 1978, Mr. Healey had got things right, but again the Labour government without a parliamentary majority was unable to keep incomes under control.

The outcome was that Mrs. Thatcher chose an entirely different path. Her solution to the stagflation problem was to intensify the contraction of the economy with the intention of removing inflationary expectations more rapidly. Part and parcel of that was supposed to be a reduction in the public sector, leaving room for a private sector-led upswing. Originally, incomes policy was not going to be part of this. This was changed in 1980 when it became apparent that cash limits and control of the money supply required some form of income restraint for the public sector. This is still in existence and is not to be abandoned for the forseeable future. (It is perfectly obvious that since wages of public employees are such an important part of public expenditure, they must be controlled in some way if that expenditure is to be limited.)

The inflation rate has also risen in this most recent period for several reasons. One is the rise in VAT and the attempt to switch the tax burden away from direct taxes and towards indirect ones. The second is pressure on nationalised industries to improve their financial performance. When they are subject to great rises in costs, this means an increase in their prices. Thirdly, restrictive monetary policy has been associated with higher rates of interest which are again reflected in costs and prices. Fourthly, as we have noted, there was a new bout of wage push in 1979—80 which only began to abate in 1981. All of these kept the inflation rate in double figures and made it hard to reduce inflationary expectations and bring the inflation rate down to the kind of levels experienced in the 1960s. In 1983, at long last, the inflation rate has been reduced to the mean of that earlier period—with unemployment six times as high.

Although we have discussed inflation and referred to trade unions and incomes policy, we have not examined the behaviour of wages in any detail. In Table 5.4 we give figures for the percentage change in wage rates and earnings, which are then plotted in Figures 5.3 and 5.4. Both series move in much the same way and the correlation between them is 0.97. (It may be added that each series is highly correlated with the index of consumer prices, the correlation coefficient being 0.9.)

The story of these series is much the same as that for inflation in general — wage rate increases, for example, staying in lowish figures for the 1960s. There is a slight upward trend with a distinct acceleration in 1968. A much more powerful boost occurs in 1970, and from then on earnings rise in double figures for every year, wage rates doing the same except for

Table 5.4 Percentage Change in Wage Rates and Earnings

	Wage Rates	Earnings
1963	3.7	4.9
1964	4.8	7.0
1965	4.3	6.8
1966	4.6	6.4
1967	3.9	6.2
1968	6.6	7.8
1969	5.3	7.2
1970	9.9	12.9
1971	12.9	11.3
1972	13.8	13.0
1973	13.7	13.1
1974	19.8	20.6
1975	29.5	29.0
1976	19.3	14.7
1977	6.6	10.0
1978	14.1	13.9
1979	15.0	15.9
1980	18.0	20.0
1981	10.2	12.9
1982	6.9	9.4

1970. Moreover, from 1970 onwards, wage rates more or less accelerate in every year except 1976 and 1977. (There was also, of course, a deceleration in 1981.)

In analysing causation, it may be hypothesised that consumer prices influence wage claims, and wages paid influence costs, and, therefore, consumer prices. For this reason it is extremely difficult to disentangle what causes what. The problem is made even more difficult if there are other economic forces influencing both wages and consumer prices. A slackness of trade will manifest itself in both goods and labour markets, for example. Similarly, an external factor may cause employers and wage earners to change their expectations in similar ways. For example, a rise in the price of oil may affect prices simply because firms anticipate a rise in their costs. It may also affect wages because workers anticipate a rise in prices.

Ignoring external factors for the moment, a possible

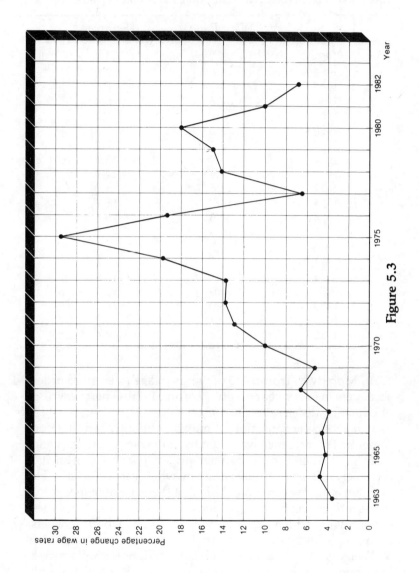

Figure 5.3

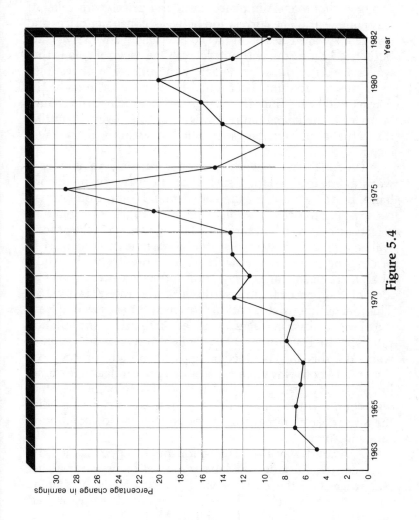

Figure 5.4

theory to account for wage—price interaction would be, firstly, to argue that wages influence costs and prices with a lag of (say) one year. (The correlation between consumer prices and last year's wage rates is, in fact, 0.8.) Wages, themselves, are influenced by prices without delay. One view of this is that wages are set to offset immediately the change in prices, plus or minus an amount determined by what it is thought the market will bear. Since the change in wages minus the change in prices is the change in real wages, another way of putting this is that real wages are determined by what the market will bear.

We can then see a wage—price spiral arising in a number of ways. Some external force such as an oil price rise, on the one hand, or an increase in aggregate demand, on the other, may cause prices to rise. This will be fed into wages, which in turn affects prices, which in turn affects wages again. This process will go on indefinitely unless either the whole of an increase in prices is not transmitted to wages, or, more likely, the whole of an increase in wages is not transmitted to prices. To get an idea of the process, suppose the inflation rate rises by 1%. This means that wage inflation rates rise by 1% as well. If (say) 0.8 of the increase in wages are added on to prices, the inflation rate will rise by another 0.8%, which in turn is added on to wages. Of this, 0.64 is added on to prices, and the process continues until both wage rate increase and price inflation increases have risen by 5%. Of course, the point also holds the other way round. If the inflation rate is lowered, this may modify the rate of rise of money wages, leading to yet a lower inflation rate and so on.

A second way the wage spiral might appear is if (say) wage earners misjudge the labour market or press for higher real wages, on the basis of an assumed greater bargaining strength. If this extra push is also transmitted at least in part into prices, the same kind of spiral as before will emerge.

Questions

1.   A price index is constructed by taking a sample of household's expenditure to determine the relative importance

of various items of expenditure. The percentage change in these items is then multiplied by these 'weights', or measures of relative importance to give the average increase in prices. How would you construct a price index for the sorts of things you buy? Why might one person's price index differ from another's, and from the published index of retail prices?

2. We have pointed out that both unemployment and inflation appear to be subject to some kind of ratchet effect. Every time they exceed their past peak it becomes harder to get them down again. Why might this be so? Could the two ratchets be interconnected? What additional information might help you to clarify the problem?

3. The Phillips curve postulated that the lower the unemployment level the faster money wages would rise. Another view is that the faster money wages rise the higher will be unemployment. How would you justify either hypothesis? Could both be true? If both were true, could the separate forces at work be disentangled from the data?

4. It has been said of OPEC that as a monopolist it will cause a once-for-all rise in the price of what it sells, but not a continuous inflation. How might this view be criticised? More generally, what is the connection between monopoly and inflation? It is apparent that the UK economy was more monopolistic in the 1970s than earlier. Could this account for stagflation, that is the increase in inflation *and* unemployment?

5. Inflation expectations are referred to in the text. How would you measure them? Under what circumstances might inflation expectations differ from recent experience of inflation?

6. What factors limit the divergence of a country's inflation rate from the world average?

7. It is argued by some economists that a faster inflation rate is determined solely by a more rapid increase in the money supply. Other economists say that the more rapid increase in the money supply is caused by the faster infla-

tion rate. As in Question 3, can you separate the two
views, and disentangle their relative importance?

8. Following Question 7, consider a rise in VAT. Does this
add to the inflation rate because it is passed on in higher
prices? Does it lower the inflation rate because real effective demand is lower? Does it lower the inflation rate
because the government would have more tax revenue
(and smaller budget deficit) and would not have the same
need to increase the money supply? Given all this, if the
Chancellor of the Exchequer's objective in 1979—80 was
to lower the inflation rate, should he have raised VAT so
drastically?

6

The Balance of Payments

The balance of payments records the transactions between the UK economy and the rest of the world which take place in a given period. The discussion of national income in Chapter 1 has already involved us in a consideration of the receipts from exports of goods and services and the payments for imports. Also included in national income is net property income from abroad, that is the income from rent, interest, profits and dividends received by UK residents from overseas *less* the corresponding item of income paid to overseas residents from activity in the UK. In addition there are transfer payments made by households and governments to foreigners, or received by them from foreigners. (There are also adjustments to be made to account for UK payments of foreign taxes and foreign payments of UK taxes.) These transfers may be gifts made by a British family to its relatives overseas. Much more important than that sort of thing in recent years have been overseas aid and the payments made by the government to such bodies as the European Community.

The Balance of Payments on Current Account includes figures for the export and import of goods and services, property income, and current transfers. In Table 6.1 the relevant figures are given for 1982. Before interpreting this, and especially the last line for the current balance, something must be said about the process of importing and exporting.

A UK importer in obtaining goods from abroad will pay for them by running down his bank account at home, or abroad (if he has one), or by borrowing at home, or by borrowing abroad. (Included in the last of these is the possibility that the

Table 6.1 Balance of Payments on Current Account, £m

	1979	1982
Exports	40,687	55,565
Imports	44,136	53,181
Trade Balance	(−3,449)	(2,384)
Services	4,071	3,874
Interest, Profits Dividends	1,090	1,402
Transfers	−2,265	−2,109
Invisibles	(2,896)	(3,167)
Current Balance	−553	5,551

foreign exporter from whom he buys will extend some trade credit to him for a while, but this is on the assumption, of course, that proper payment will be made after that.)

Whatever method the importer uses, there is also the problem of whether he pays in sterling or in a foreign currency (say) dollars. If he pays in dollars, and has no dollar account, he will use the sterling he has (or can borrow) to purchase dollars which he will then transmit abroad. It may be, however, that the foreign exporter will be content to receive a cheque in sterling. He could then exchange this for dollars at his own bank, or he may credit it to his UK bank account, if he has one.

What is important to appreciate is that, except for the intervention of foreign currency, there is no difference between this kind of transaction and that between a domestic buyer of goods and a domestic seller. In other words, ignoring the usual possibility of bankruptcy (which is not confined to foreign transactions), and bearing in mind that trade credit means that there will be a short delay in completing some transactions, imports are paid for in much the same way as any other kind of transaction.

This discussion of UK imports has already mentioned the foreign exporter. It is obvious that the case of UK exports is exactly the same with the roles reversed. The UK exporter may extend credit for a while, but eventually will be paid in sterling or overseas currency, and as far as the latter is concerned, will hold it for a while (especially if he is an importer as well) or will convert it into sterling.

Once again, the key point is that he is paid. It follows that, when the sum total of exports is calculated and compared with the sum total of imports, while these figures may differ, that does not mean that either UK or foreign exporters have been done out of their money. What then does it mean?

We have seen already that an importer pays for his transactions by running down his bank account, or borrowing abroad. In other words, his financial assets are reduced. An exporter adds to his bank account or lends abroad. His financial assets are increased. We may then see in the same way that a net flow of property income from abroad involves the transfer of foreign assets to UK citizens. Similarly, grants made by households or governments to foreigners implies a rundown in their assets.

It is now easy to summarise and say that a surplus on the current account of the balance of payments means that international inflows exceed international outflows; and that this represents a net increase in the overall UK assets position. Similarly, a current account deficit implies a net decrease in the UK asset position. (A surplus on current account is then *defined* as a country's net foreign investment.)

There are two additional aspects of this which must be emphasised. One is that the current account reflects both private sector and public sector transactions. It is possible, therefore, for the private sector to be in surplus (and acquiring net assets) while the public sector is in deficit to such an extent that the overall account is in deficit.

Secondly, suppose the current account is in deficit. The net payment to be made to foreigners might be acceptable in sterling. If it is not, UK residents must acquire dollars. They may borrow them, but if they are unable to do that, they may obtain them from their banks, who in turn may obtain dollars from dealers in foreign exchange. They may acquire such dollars from the Bank of England. If that does not happen, sterling ending up in the hands of foreigners will flow into their banks, then into their central bank, which in turn may demand the equivalent amount of dollars from the Bank of England. Either way, at the going rate of exchange, the Bank of

England's reserves of foreign currency will fall. Alternatively, they will have to sell some of the foreign assets they own or themselves borrow abroad. This is, broadly speaking, what happens if Britain wishes to keep to a fixed rate of exchange (i.e. it wants the value of its currency in terms of foreign currencies to stay constant).

Another way of looking at these things is to say that, if the Bank of England does not buy unwanted sterling and supply dollars at the going price of sterling, that price will fall. We may then say that there is a problem on current account if the Bank does not have the reserves to buy back unwanted sterling or can only borrow to do so on unattractive terms. It must then be added that the other possibility is to let the external value of the pound fall. To the extent that that is desirable, the tendency of the current account to move into deficit is not a problem at all. The merits of a floating exchange rate are precisely to avoid balance of payments problems by letting the currency trade at its market price, free of government intervention.

This leads us on to the capital account, which reflects the overseas borrowing and lending by households, firms and the government. A decision by a UK resident to buy shares in Germany (say) represents an outflow of sterling and the inflow of a German asset. To be offset against this may be an inflow of that money into a UK firm. In this connection a distinction is sometimes made between long-term and short-term capital account transactions. Investment by a multinational in an overseas subsidiary might be long-term, while purchase of a 90 day US Treasury Bill as an abode for a temporary acquisition of cash would be short-term.

We leave out of the capital account those transactions of an asset nature to do with movements of international reserves. In other words, we add to the net current account surplus net UK purchases of overseas assets and other external capital flows. It is this final amount that the Bank of England has to finance by running down reserves or special borrowing overseas. If that does not happen, the value of sterling will fall below what would otherwise be the case.

It is necessary to add that, just as a fall in the value of sterling may not be a problem if that is what the government

Table 6.2 Balance of Payments on Capital Account, £m

	1979	1982
Net Investment		
Overseas	1,835	−3,258
Official Financing etc.	−1,710	1,284
Balancing Items	428	−3,577
	553	−5,551

wants for other policy purposes, so a fall in reserves might be desirable. The question is whether the country has an excess of reserves, or expects them to rise in the future. Just as an individual or firm may rationally run down its assets or acquire debts to be repaid in the future, so may a country as a whole. It all depends on its objectives and the way in which present action affects future welfare.

In Table 6.2 we show the capital account for 1982 and the extent of official financing of the overall deficit. Official financing equals overall receipts minus expenditures. In order to make the two sides of the account add up, this must be written as a negative number, i.e.

Receipts − expenditure − increase in reserves = zero.

This means in the capital account that a negative number under 'official financing' corresponds to an overall surplus and an increase in reserves. (The balancing item is a statistical device to account for our inability to identify all transactions appropriately. Unhappily, this item has been rather large for the past three or four years.)

The key points to note about Table 6.1 are the following:

(a) There was a surplus of exports of goods over imports of goods in 1982. This is sometimes referred to as the visible balance, and a surplus in this has recurred for the past three years, but was last experienced in 1971.
(b) There was a surplus of exports of services over imports. This is quite usual in the UK.
(c) Net interest, profits and dividends were positive. This is

usual. (In 1980 we had the unusual experience of this part of the account being in deficit.)

(d)   A net deficit on transfers. This has grown drastically in the 1970s and is due largely to net government spending abroad, including its net contribution to the EEC. Overall, items (c) and (d) reduce a surplus in (a) and (b) of £6,258m. to a current balance of £5,551m. (Ten years ago the deficit on transfers was of the order of £300—£400m.)

Turning to Table 6.2, and bearing in mind the balancing item, what stands out for 1982 are:

(a)   The large net private investment abroad. This has risen dramatically since 1978.
(b)   The overall capital outflow.
(c)   The fall in reserves and other official financing.
(d)   The enormous balancing item.

It is worth comparing this with 1979 when the current account was in deficit to the tune of £863m. Net private investments abroad was £3,150m. Nonetheless, there was a net inward capital flow of £2,170m. and a balancing item of £403m. Thus, the balance of payments was in overall surplus by £1,710m., leading to a rise of reserves and other official financing. This shows that reserves may rise even with a current account deficit. (1979 is also interesting because, although the current account was in deficit, that part due to the private sector was in surplus.)

Let us now take a longer view. In Table 6.3 is given the current balance in the balance of payments, both in actual money terms and as a fraction of gross domestic product at market prices. It can be seen that this fluctuated between about ± £360m. in the period 1958—68. As a fraction of GDP it varied from about plus one and a half per cent to minus one per cent. These are not trivial sums, and did create serious difficulties at the time, but they can hardly be regarded as of overwhelming significance. It was true that four of the five years from 1964 were ones of deficit, and this helped to precipitate the crisis of late 1967 which was accompanied by a devaluation. Nonetheless, in retrospect that seems minor compared with the experience of the 1970s.

Table 6.3 Current Balance of the Balance of Payments

	£m.	Percentage of GDP at Market Prices	Exchange Rate $ per £	Average External Value of the £ 1975 = 100
1958	360	1.6	2.8	
1959	172	0.7	2.8	
1960	−228	−0.9	2.8	
1961	47	0.2	2.8	
1962	155	0.5	2.8	
1963	125	0.4	2.8	
1964	−358	−1.1	2.8	
1965	−30	−0.1	2.8	
1966	130	0.3	2.8	
1967	−269	−0.7	2.8	
1968	−244	−0.6	2.4	
1969	505	1.1	2.4	
1970	823	1.6	2.4	128
1971	1124	2.0	2.4	128
1972	223	0.3	2.5	124
1973	−979	−1.3	2.5	112
1974	−3,278	−3.9	2.3	108
1975	−1,513	−1.4	2.2	100
1976	−836	−0.7	1.8	86
1977	54	0.0	1.7	81
1978	1,158	0.7	1.9	82
1979	−553	−0.3	2.1	87
1980	3,650	1.6	2.3	96
1981	7,272	2.9	2.0	95
1982	5,551	2.0	1.7	91

Before considering that, it is necessary to examine 1968 to 1973. Sterling was devalued by some 14% against the dollar in November, 1967. The immediate effect of that was to make imports dearer in sterling terms and exports cheaper in dollar terms. But that did not affect demands or supplies for a while; therefore, we simply paid more for out imports. The net result, therefore, was to make the balance of payments temporarily worse. (This is the so-called J-curve effect.) It was not until 1969, therefore, that the current account went into surplus. Another reason why the benefits of devaluation were delayed is that output continued to grow rapidly in 1968. Policy measures were introduced to restrain the economy, and these led to below average expansion in 1969 and the subsequent few years. It was that restraint, coupled with devaluation, that eventually caused a balance of payments surplus.

In 1973 policy was changed. It was decided to use monetary and fiscal policies to expand the economy very rapidly. If this led to a deterioration in the balance of payments, the pound would be allowed to float and fall in value, if necessary. In other words, the reserves would not be used up or resort made to official borrowing abroad. As economic theory predicted, a large current account deficit emerged in 1973. This was three times larger in ordinary money than anything experienced before, and at -1.3% of GDP was more significant than the deficits of the 1960s. The average external value of sterling also dropped 10% between 1972 and 1973.

On top of the problems resulting from what is now recognised to have been an excessively expansive monetary and fiscal policy were two other events: (a) the first oil price explosion, and (b) the miners' strike which destroyed the Heath government and led to the wage explosion of 1974—5. Since the UK elasticity of demand for oil was less than unity, quantity demanded did not fall much as price rose. Thus, expenditure increased. With North Sea oil not yet flowing rapidly, this expenditure implied a deterioration in the current account of the balance of payments. Indeed, as the table shows, there was the largest deficit in modern history. Measured by the retail price index, the inflation rate in 1974 went for the first time into double figures. Although gross domestic product fell, the fall was not sufficient to offset the other forces. The current account remained strongly in deficit for the succeeding two years. Matters were gradually brought under control, and by 1978 there was a strong surplus. Even then an above average increase in demand in 1978 coupled with a reversal of the downward trend in inflation gave rise to yet another large deficit in 1979. It was only in 1980 that a significant surplus emerged. And that was based on the receipts from North Sea oil and the reduction in imports due to a depressed economy. The underlying balance of payments position at the end of the

1970s was almost certainly worse than that at the end of the previous decade. Nonetheless, in 1981 and 1982 the surplus became much larger still, both absolutely and as a fraction of gross domestic product. The oil price rise at the end of the decade was beneficial to Britain as an oil producer, just as the later turnround in the oil market was harmful.

It is most instructive to compare Table 6.3 in this chapter with Table 2.1 in Chapter 2 (p. 18). An examination of the two together suggests that from 1960 to 1969, if real income rose more rapidly in one year compared with the previous year, the current account of the balance of payments deteriorated. The only counter-example was 1968 when there was a slight improvement in the current account, and, of course, sterling had just been devalued. (A similar but not quite as strong proposition can be made about the relationship between the rate of increase of money income and the balance of payments.)

In the subsequent decade the connection is much weaker and hardly exists at all. Whether or not the current account improved, depended on forces other than, or in addition to, the buoyancy of output. The obvious ones are oil prices and the flow of North Sea oil on the one hand, and cost-push inflation on the other. The latter is not to be treated entirely separately from the effects of demand. A deterioration in the balance of payments may arise because aggregate demand increases relative to aggregate supply from domestic sources. The difference is then made up from sources abroad.

One reason why demand may be diverted abroad is a taste for foreign goods. It must always be recognised, however, that preference must be considered relative to price. What is necessary to improve matters, therefore, is that relative prices must shift to divert home demand away from goods that might be exported as well as from imports. In addition, production must shift towards producing such exportables. In other words, there must be a rise in the relative price of what may be exported (and of potential imports). This will divert demand away from them, and supply towards them. In addition, this rise in price must be an increase relative to costs, notably wage costs, so as to make the extra production profitable.

It follows that, if wages rise relative to prices in industries that export or compete with imports, and productivity does not increase to offset this, supply will fall. The result will be a worsening in the balance of payments, unless the fall in prices is offset by a devaluation of the currency. One explanation of the behaviour of the balance of payments (net of North Sea oil) since the mid-1970s is precisely such a rise in costs relative to price. Given the respective qualities of goods, foreigners are able to penetrate our markets because their prices (and therefore their costs) are lower than ours, for what they offer. An excessive tendency to import is a supply problem as well as a demand one.

To take a longer view of the problem, Table 6.3 also contains figures for the value of sterling in terms of dollars, and for the value of sterling relative to foreign currencies in general. (The latter is sometimes called the *effective* exchange rate. The exchange rate may be thought of as (i) how much foreign currency sterling will buy (e.g. $1.4 for each £), or (ii) the purchase price of foreign currency (e.g. $1 cost 71p). Up to the beginning of the 1970s the £ was fixed in value. This meant that the Bank of England endeavoured to stabilise the price at $2.8 to £1 up to 1967 and $2.4 to £1 after the devaluation of that year. To do so they bought up at the going rate all excess pounds that foreigners did not want, and supplied all the sterling that foreigners wanted at that rate if it were not available from other sources.

Since neither Britain's reserves nor her borrowing powers were unlimited, domestic policy had to be adjusted to deal with a current account deficit. Demand had to be cut somewhat to reduce excessive expenditure and to bring inflation in line with that of the rest of the world. The inflation objective was also approached by means of incomes policies. The dilemma for policy makers was whether the domestic restraint necessary to achieve the balance of payments objective did not also damp down productive activity too much. If it did, unemployment would be too high on average and the growth rate too low. Although this was a major worry at the time, as Chapters 2, 4 and 9 show, the growth performance was better then than now, and unemployment very much lower and less intractable. Nonetheless, it was still necessary to admit defeat in 1967 and accept that the $ parity could no longer be maintained. Sterling was devalued but to a new lower *fixed* rate.

The policy was also eventually reinforced by still greater cuts of demand. This was something of a paradox considering that the objective was to free us from the balance of payments constraint!

In 1973 a different tack was tried. Sterling was to be allowed to float free. Its price would be what it would bring in the open market. An excess supply of sterling resulting from a balance of payments deficit would cause its external value to fall. Excess demand would cause its external value to rise. Supposedly, the Bank of England would stay out of the market except to smooth day-to-day changes in the rate, and lower the risks of foreign trading.

As a result, from 1973 onwards the average external value of sterling fell. (It rose for a while against the dollar which had troubles of its own, but soon fell against that as well.) Sterling in a free market also had a greater tendency to fluctuate. From 1977 onwards it rose fairly rapidly, reaching a peak in 1981 before falling once again.

What is also of interest is the connection (or lack of connection) between the external value of sterling and the balance of payments on current account. From 1974 onwards, the current balance was in deficit and the external value of sterling fell. But the size of the fall was not directly related to the size of the deficit. Moreover, in 1979 the deficit worsened and the pound rose in value. In 1981 there was a massive surplus, but the dollar exchange rate fell and the effective exchange rate did not rise. This is not surprising, for, as we have said, the relevant consideration is the overall balance of payments. If, for example, there is a net capital inflow, this may offset a current account deficit. Such an inflow may occur as a result of UK interest rates being high relative to the rest of the world's, or because sterling is *expected* to become scarcer, or because holding sterling is thought to be less risky than holding other currencies.

In 1977 there was a large inflow of funds and a rise in reserves, so that the fall in sterling was arrested. Although there was a current surplus in 1978, the capital inflow was checked so that sterling rose in value, but only slowly. In 1979, despite the current deficit, a great deal of foreign capital flowed in so that sterling rose even more. Finally, in 1980–82 a strong influence was the current account surplus, but there were also major capital outflows. It should also be appreciated that the abolition of exchange control in 1979 in a curious way added at least temporarily to confidence in sterling. The fact that the government was confident enough to remove restraints on UK residents' ability to invest abroad very much impressed foreign investors. (There is, however, a heavy price to pay for this if and when there is a run on the pound.) The effect did not endure, however. The abolition of exchange control allowed funds to flow out of the UK whenever investors felt that somewhere else (notably New York) was a safer or more profitable abode for their funds.

In sum, it is a mistake to assume that there is a close and immediate connection between the current account of the balance of payments and the exchange rate. The current account may be in surplus, but the average value of the pound abroad falls or stays about the same. Examples would be 1972 and 1978 and 1981. Moreover, the current account may be in deficit but the average value of the pound rises as in 1979.

Let us now examine two other matters. One is the question of how competitive the UK has been relative to suppliers overseas. The other concerns the behaviour of the current account minus the trade in oil. The two are interdependent in that it may be hypothesised that a decline in competitiveness will lead to a fall in exports and a rise in imports of manufacturers and semi-manufacturers of all kinds.

We have already suggested that the propensity to export will depend on how profitable that activity is. This might be measured by the price received for exports relative to costs and notably wage costs. The price of exports is, of course, the price charged in sterling times the rate of exchange expressed as overseas currency per pound. A fall in the external value of the pound will, other things being equal, make UK exports appear more attractive to foreign importers. A fall in their UK price relative to the costs of producing them, while that might increase foreign demand, may reduce supply in total, including that part going overseas.

In Table 6.4 and Figure 6.1 figures are given for relative export prices and the relative profitability of exports. The first

Table 6.4 Relative Export Prices and the Relative Profitability of Exports (1980 = 100)

	Relative Export Prices	Relative Profitability of Exports	Import Price Competitiveness
1963	83		
1964	83		
1965	85		
1966	87		
1967	86		
1968	81		
1969	80		
1970	81	103	94
1971	83	99	98
1972	83	98	99
1973	77	101	93
1974	75	101	89
1975	78	103	92
1976	76	104	88
1977	80	106	89
1978	85	105	88
1979	90	106	95
1980	100	100	100
1981	98	101	101
1982	93	102	98
1983	92	106	92

of these measures shows in broad terms how UK prices of these tradeable manufactured goods look compared with those of foreign exports of the same sorts of things. The second compares export prices and wholesale prices of home sales of manufactures. It does not, therefore, reflect the profitability of manufacturing as such, but only how well production for overseas compares with production for the domestic market.

Looking at the two series from 1970 onwards, what is noteworthy is how the relative price series fluctuates so much more than the relative profitability series. This is not surprising since the former largely reflects the latter plus the additional factors of the rate of exchange and foreign prices. Although

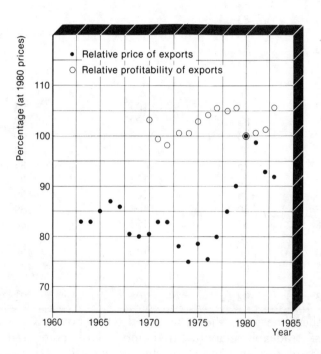

Figure 6.1

there is not a close statistical relationship between the two series, what there is seems to be a negative one. This is compatible with the view that, if relative export prices alter because of variations in the exchange rate, some of that change is offset by also changing the sterling price of exports.

On the relative price of exports, it can be seen how this was tending to rise before the 1967 devaluation. There was then a fall, but it was rather less than the extent of the devaluation. In other words, as economic theory would predict, because a devaluation implies a rise in foreign demand, exporters raised their price somewhat in sterling terms. (Prices rose in sterling terms because of a rise in money wages as well.)

Competitiveness remained fairly stable until the expansion of 1973. The average external value of sterling fell drastically in 1973 and 1974. This lowered the relative price of exports even though UK inflation was increasing rapidly. It is also worth noting that the relative profitability of exports which fell from 1970 to 1972 then started to increase.

What is specially interesting, however, are the events of the three years 1978—1980. The relative prices of exports rose, following in large part the increase in the exchange rate. This went hand in hand with a significant fall in the profitability of exports. Since 1980 exports have been becoming more competitive and more profitable. It may also be added that the relative price of imports has fallen since 1981 by about 8%.

In Table 6.5 we give the figures for the volume of exports and imports of manufactured goods in the last half of the 1970s and early 1980s. What is most startling is the rise in the volume of manufactured imports by 75% in seven years. By contrast, the volume of exports has risen only by 13%. The recovery of 1982 has not restored the position of three years earlier. Once again it is necessary to refer back to the figures of real output growth of Chapter 2, Table 2.1. Gross domestic product in 1982 was some 8% higher than in 1975, but imports of manufactured goods were 75% higher.

Putting the pieces together, it is apparent that maintaining the volume of exports of manufacturers has been a remarkable achievement. After all, the average value of sterling rose in the period and export competition fell. From 1977 onwards the relative profitability of exporting also fell. Presumably,

Table 6.5 Volume of Exports and Imports of Manufactured Goods (1980 = 100)

	Exports	Imports
1975	85	66
1976	93	72
1977	100	79
1978	99	88
1979	99	101
1980	100	100
1981	94	107
1982	96	115

however, given the state of the home market, it was better to sell abroad than not at all. It is on the imports side that the puzzle remains. Obviously, imports became more competitive by about 12%, but, given the low rate of expansion of gross domestic product, that is hardly enough to account for the rise in import volume. This must be due to an inability and unwillingness of UK industry to compete in its own markets. One cause may be a rise in wage costs and another may be lack of investment in manufacturing capacity. We return to these themes in Chapter 9 on economic growth.

Questions

1. Consider a UK importer buying goods from the US. Suppose he agrees a price fixed in dollars. Assume in addition that delivery takes time (say, three months). What sort of risks does he run concerning the amount of sterling he is committed to? Is there anything he can do to reduce those risks?

2. A current account deficit may lead to a loss of reserves. If reserves are scarce, eventually the exchange rate may be devalued. Given that, how might expectations about the future exchange rate be determined? Suppose there is speculation based on those expectations. How might that affect the reserves and the actual exchange rate?

3. Extend our discussion of the balance of payments to clarify precisely what is meant by a balance of payments problem. Can an overall surplus be a problem? In what sense is the problem one for households and firms? Is a balance of payments problem entirely a government matter?

4. We have suggested that there may be a connection between increases in income (real or money) and deterioration in the balance of payments. Would this necessarily apply to both the current and capital accounts? What other information would you need to distinguish the effects on the two accounts?

5. It could be argued that an increase in exports leads to an improved balance of payments and higher real income. This is the reverse of the case discussed in the text and in Question 4. What extra information would help you determine whether this phenomenon ever occurs?

6. If sterling is left free to find its market value, how would expectations about that value be determined? How exactly would you expect the exchange rate to reflect differences between UK and foreign inflation rates?

7. How would you set about discovering whether the rise in UK manufacturing imports since the mid-1970s was due to a rise in the foreign propensity to export, rather than a rise in the UK propensity to import?

7

Money

The UK economy is a monetary economy. This means simply that the overwhelming majority of transactions take place via the mechanism of money. Buyers buy with money or receive credit. Sellers sell for money or extend credit. In the case of credit this is only a temporary expedient. Except for deliberate fraud and bankruptcy, eventually the completion of a transaction involves the transfer of money from a buyer to a lender. It would be surprising if in such an economy money were to be shown to be unimportant. But, in arguing for the significance of money, a macroeconomist is not saying that money is all that matters for an understanding of the economy. Money matters, but it is not the only thing that matters.

Oddly enough, although economists agree that money has to be taken seriously, it cannot be said that the questions, 'what is money?', and, 'how is the quantity of money to be measured?', have yet been answered satisfactorily.

Money is often defined as a medium of exchange. It avoids the use of barter and facilitates the division of labour. The typical transactions are, as we have said, from goods into money or from money into goods. If money is a medium of exchange, then it might be said that every medium of exchange is money. In that case it follows that credit of every kind must be included in the quantity of money.

However, because a credit transaction is not final, it is usually stated that money should be defined more narrowly as a means of payment. In other words, whatever is given over by the buyer, which the seller regards as ending the transaction, is money. (Since this definition would allow whatever is given in the occasional barter transaction to be regarded as money, perhaps the word 'usually' should be added.) The means of payment definition of money would limit it nearly entirely to notes and coins and cheques drawn or drawable on accounts at the banks.

It will be recalled from the theory textbooks that there are supposedly three motives that households and firms have for holding a stock of money. These are the transactions, precautionary, and speculative motives. The transactions motive arises from the difference in timing between normal receipts and payments. The household, for example, receives an income at the beginning of every week or month and disperses most of it in the next seven or thirty days. Since it is too much trouble to invest the unspent receipts for very short periods of time, money balances are held to facilitate everyday transactions. The argument applies less forcibly to firms, especially large ones, who will find it profitable to be highly economical in their money holdings. But even they will hold some transactions balances.

Over and above ordinary transactions, because receipts are not 100% certain, and possible purchases even less so, households and firms will hold precautionary balances. They are a kind of safety allowance against unforeseen trading contingencies. As opposed to normal transactions balances, they might be defined as abnormal transactions balances.

Households and firms are also interested in holding assets of various kinds. These yield returns which may be certain or involve a degree of risk. The interest on national savings is paid for certain, as is that on government bonds. The dividend on industrial ordinary shares is much less certain. In addition to the riskiness of returns, there is also the possibility in some cases of capital gains and losses. Because of antipathy to risk, investors, in determining the composition of their portfolios of assets, will hold some of their wealth in relatively riskless form. This may also be in short-term, fixed interest government bonds with little capital variation, notably Treasury Bills, which are specially relevant to firms of various kinds. Since all these financial assets are extremely liquid, they fulfil the speculative motive (which is sometimes actually called the liquidity motive). It is, indeed, not obvious why the speculative motive will ever be met willingly by holding cash or a bank account. By chance or because financial transactions cannot be undertaken costlessly or instantaneously, there will be a speculative demand for cash and current accounts. But this must be small and temporary.

If now money is defined as whatever meets the transactions, precautionary, and speculative motives, it will include an extremely wide range of assets. This will be wider either than the medium of exchange or the means of payment. In particular, it will include a great many assets on which interest is paid.

Given this background it is apparent why economists and policy makers work with at least two definitions of the money supply. The first is called M1. It includes notes and coins held by the public plus current accounts in the banks held by households and firms in the private sector. The second is called sterling M3. In addition to M1 it includes all sterling deposits held by UK residents (in both public and private sectors). In other words, it defines as money some financial assets on which interest is earned. Nonetheless, M3 is a relevant measure if the precautionary and speculative motives are to begin to be covered. Even that, however, is not satisfactory as a medium of exchange. It leaves out credit, especially trade credit, which is the basis of a large number of transactions in the economy. Without such credit, currency and current accounts would have to take on more of the medium of exchange functions. Thus, they would be less able to fulfil the other functions of money.

As far as elementary theory is concerned, it is argued that the demand for a means of payment and a medium of exchange is closely connected with the level of money national income. To put the point another way, taking money income as one factor determining the demand for money covers much of the transactions and precautionary motives. To the extent that money is demanded as an asset, it could be argued that the relevant variables would be the wealth of the private sector and the interest rate. The wealthier people are, the more they wish to hold money as an asset. The higher the interest rate, the more expensive it is to hold non-interest bearing money.

In Table 7.1 are given the figures for the ratio of M1 and

M3 to gross domestic product at current prices. The figures are plotted in Figure 7.1. Although there is a slight cyclical quality about the M1 series, what is most remarkable about it is its steady downwards trend. The inverse of this ratio is the income velocity of circulation of money. Thus, another way of putting the same point is to say that there is a steady upwards trend in velocity.

The behaviour of M3 is rather different. This series has a much greater degree of variation. This is especially true of the cycle between 1971 and 1975. Also, having shown a trend fall up to 1980, it has now risen quite significantly.

Nonetheless, it is apparent that both firms and households have become much more economical in their use of money over these two decades. The velocity of M1 has risen by 50% over the period. One possible reason for this is the growth of money substitutes such as credit cards. A second might be a rise in the interest forgone from holding money. As Table 7.1 shows, if the relevant interest rate is long term, as measured, for example, by the yield on long-dated government stocks, that has certainly risen over the period. This argument, however, does not apply to M3 since it includes interest-earning deposits. Presumably, the interest part of M3 has been rising partly to offset the fall in the M1 ratio. Indeed, it may explain why M1 has fallen so much relative to M3, from about 2/3 of it in 1963 to only 2/5 in 1982.

What is worth explaining is the connection between changes in the money stock, however measured, and changes in the two components of GDP at current prices, namely GDP at constant prices and the price level. The annual percentage changes in M1 and M3 have themselves varied considerably in this period. They are plotted in Figure 7.2 and show some odd characteristics.

Up to 1972, although the percentage change in sterling M3 always exceeded the percentage change in M1, the two series moved very much in line. It follows that those economic theories and predictions which placed great emphasis on changes in the money supply, would not be too sensitive to which series was used. From 1973 onwards the position has been quite different. In eight of the ten years the two series have moved in opposite directions. In four cases M1 has

Table 7.1 The Money Supply

	M1 as a Percentage of GDP at Current Prices	Annual Percentage Change in M1	Sterling M3 as a Percentage of GDP at Current Prices	Annual Percentage Change in Sterling M3	Velocity of Circulation of: M1	Velocity of Circulation of: M3	Treasury Bill Yield	Long-Dated Government Security Yield	Percentage Change in M1 minus the Percentage Change in Prices	Percentage Change in M3 minus the Percentage Change in Prices
1963	24		37		4.2	2.7	3.8	5.6		
1964	22	3.3	36	5.8	4.5	2.8	6.7	6.0	-0.3	2.2
1965	21	2.1	35	6.6	4.8	2.9	5.6	6.6	-3.3	1.2
1966	20	-0.1	34	3.3	5.0	2.9	6.6	6.6	-4.3	-0.9
1967	20	8.1	36	9.8	5.0	2.8	7.6	6.9	5.0	6.7
1968	20	5.2	36	8.1	5.0	2.9	6.9	7.6	0.9	3.8
1969	19	0.2	34	2.1	5.3	2.9	7.8	9.1	-5.2	-3.3
1970	18	8.8	34	9.4	5.6	2.9	6.9	9.3	1.7	-2.3
1971	18	11.6	34	12.9	5.6	2.9	4.5	8.9	2.4	3.7
1972	19	16.5	39	26.6	5.3	2.6	8.5	9.0	8.1	18.2
1973	18	6.5	43	27.2	5.6	2.3	12.8	10.8	-0.7	20.0
1974	17	11.0	42	10.2	5.9	2.4	11.3	14.8	-3.8	-4.6
1975	16	19.0	35	6.7	6.3	2.9	10.9	14.4	-8.1	-20.4
1976	15	10.0	32	8.9	6.7	3.1	14.0	14.4	-4.9	-6.0
1977	16	21.8	31	10.1	6.3	3.2	6.4	12.7	7.9	-3.8
1978	16	16.7	31	15.2	6.3	3.2	11.9	12.5	5.7	4.2
1979	15	9.1	31	12.8	6.3	3.2	16.5	13.0	-5.4	-1.7
1980	14	4.0	30	19.1	7.1	3.3	13.6	13.8	-15.8	-0.7
1981	13	10.5	34	13.3	7.7	2.9	15.4	14.8	-1.1	1.7
1982	14	12.2	34	9.7	7.1	2.9	10.0	12.9	5.0	2.5

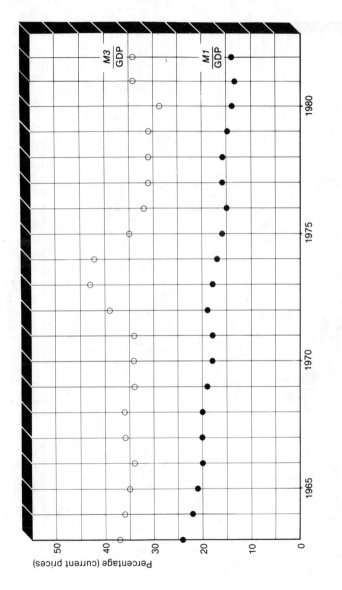

Figure 7.1

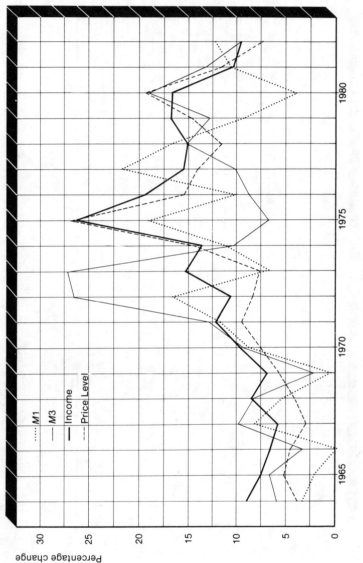

Figure 7.2

grown less rapidly and M3 more rapidly, while in four years the reverse happened. It is also worth noting that in 1974 the rate of increase of M3 was less than the rate of increase of M1, and that this state of affairs persisted until 1978. From 1979–81, M3 grew more rapidly than M1, but that was reversed again in 1982. Thirdly, of course, both series grew at much faster rates after 1973 than before.

In noting these phenomena there are four background considerations to remember. One is the coincidence of the Barber boom and the oil price rise of 1973. The next is the stagflation of the remainder of the 1970s. Thirdly, during this period much greater emphasis has been placed on monetary policy. Fourthly, methods of controlling the system of money and banking have constantly changed in a rather experimental fashion.

The Barber boom and the need to accommodate at least partially the cost-push inflation associated with the oil price rise led to the increase in the rate of expansion of the money supply. Having to continue to accommodate the resulting stagflation has caused such higher rates of increase to persist.

Secondly, a policy of tightening the money supply will be counteracted in a market system by those who demand money and find it scarce. It will pay those who supply money to find a way round the tightening. Thus, in years in which M1 is held back, there will be a tendency to switch into assets comprising M3. Only if the government is able to control both series very precisely can this effect be avoided.

Turning now to the relationship between the money supply and income and prices, up to about 1971 the series appeared to move somewhat together, possibly with a lag of money income on the money supply. In the 1970s as a whole, however, the connection between changes in M1 and changes in money income seem pretty tenuous. This is true whether the series are lagged one or two years or not at all. On this experience it is hard to predict the path of money income from the path of the money supply. The position is not much better when changes in M1 are compared with changes in the price level. The best that can be said is that in six years out of ten, the two series moved in the same direction. The proposition that changes in the inflation rate can easily be predicted from earlier changes in the money supply is not supported on the basis of the behaviour of M1.

The position with M3 is somewhat better. In this case the best connection is with a two-year lag. In six years out of ten, changes in the rate of increase of sterling M3 were followed by changes in the inflation rate, and in the rate of increase of money national income. In Figure 7.3 we show the figures for the inflation rate and the change in sterling M3 of two years earlier. From 1972 onwards the two series do seem to move together, suggesting at least the possibility of a causal relationship. (Incidentally, if there is a causal relationship, the behaviour of M3 in 1979 and 1980 implies a fall in the inflation rate in 1981 and a rise in 1982.) Alternatively, whatever else is influencing the inflation rate may be connected with M3, or be signalled by it.

Let us now examine what is happening to the real money supply. The obvious way to measure this is to compare the percentage change in M1 or M3 with the inflation rate. The figures are given in the last two columns of Table 7.1. What is interesting about them is firstly the point already discussed, namely that real balances measured in terms of M1 differ from real balances measured in terms of M3. Thus, it is very hard to say in any year in the 1970s whether monetary policy was tight or loose. The most obvious differences occur in 1973, 1977, and 1980. Subject to those differences, the question arises whether changes in real balances go hand-in-hand with changes in the general level of economic activity. If Table 7.1 is compared with Table 2.1, the matter can be put to the test. It will be seen that up to the early seventies there is a possible connection between the rate of change of real money balances and the movement of real gross domestic product. The position from 1972 onwards is as always more complicated. The money supply rose relative to the inflation rate in 1972, without much immediate impact on output. The boom in 1973 coincided with a rise in real M3 and a fall in real M1. Next, real output rose pretty rapidly in 1976, with no immediate preceding or coincidental rise in real money balances. Lastly, the fall in real output in 1980 might be explained by a fall in real M1 but hardly by that in real M3, which actually rose in 1980, and did not fall a lot in 1979. The recovery in 1982 is

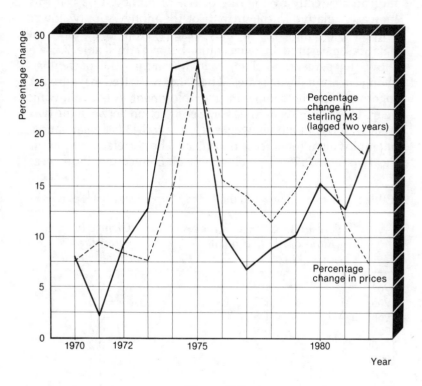

Figure 7.3

associated with a rise in real M1 and M3, the former being more substantial than the latter. It remains to question, however, what caused what.

There is one final possibility to look at. Cost push may be indicated directly by the rate of rise of money wages. If this increases relative to the growth of the money supply, lower output and employment may result. How then did real balances measured in wage units behave? In Table 7.2 we show the percentage changes in M3 minus the percentage change in annual wage rates. The data are plotted in Figure 7.4 together with the change in unemployment in the following year. There does seem to be some connection between the two (that is, a rise in money wages relative to M3 last year causes unemployment to increase this year). The correlation between the two is -0.75. The closeness of connection, however,

Table 7.2 Annual Changes in the Money Supply and Unemployment

	Percentage Change in the Ratio of M3 to Annual Wage Rates	Change in Percentage Unemployment
1964	1.0	−0.6
1965	2.3	−0.3
1966	−1.3	0.1
1967	5.9	0.8
1968	1.5	0.2
1969	−3.2	−0.1
1970	−0.5	0.2
1971	0	0.8
1972	12.8	0.3
1973	13.5	−1.1
1974	−9.6	0
1975	−22.8	1.3
1976	−10.4	1.4
1977	3.5	0.5
1978	1.1	−0.1
1979	−2.2	−0.4
1980	1.1	1.5
1981	3.1	3.7
1982	2.8	1.7

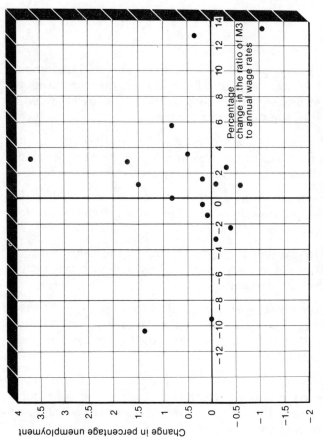

Note: 1975 data are not included; they lie outside this range

Figure 7.4

should not be exaggerated. Unemployment fell in 1973 and
rose in 1980 by more than this relationship would predict.
More significantly, the rapid rise in unemployment in 1981
and 1982 cannot be explained in this way. In other words, in
key years there will obviously be other factors at work.

Questions

1. Should accounts held by UK firms abroad and domestic
    holdings of foreign cash be included in the money supply?
    Is the demand for money in the UK to be regarded as
    equal to the supply of UK money?

2. If money gets scarcer, how will this affect the amount
    held for transactions and precautionary purposes? How
    can the use of money for such purposes be more efficient?

3. Suppose inflation is a cost of holding money. How will
    the demand for money be affected by people being more
    certain of the inflation rate?

4. Discuss further the apparent rise in the velocity of cir-
    culation of money. What other measureable factors
    might have influenced it?

5. We have noted in the text that some economists place
    great emphasis on controlling the money supply as a way
    of dealing with inflation. What difficulties can you see in
    doing this?

6. How would you pursue further the alleged connection
    between changes in the money supply and subsequent
    changes in the inflation rate? If households and firms
    recognised this connection, how would it affect their
    behaviour? What then might happen to the relationship?

7. If the rise in unemployment in the early 1980s is not at-
    tributable to too slow a growth in the money supply
    relative to money wages, what other explanations need
    to be considered? Would the behaviour of the exchange
    rate be worth examining?

8
Public Expenditure and Taxation

Both of these topics have appeared in earlier chapters. We have explained the distinction between the government's current expenditure on goods and services, and its investment expenditure. Within the latter, gross domestic capital formation by nationalised industries was separated out from the remainder. Moreover, all of these forms of expenditure were distinguished from transfer payments.

Turning to taxation, the main division of the global sum is between direct taxes and indirect taxes. Typical of the former is the income tax, and of the latter, VAT. Indeed, the relevant distinction might be better expressed as that between taxes on income and taxes on expenditure.

Our purpose in this chapter is to explore what has happened to public expenditure and taxation. Before setting out the relevant figures, it is useful to remind ourselves that the role of government activity is a broad one, and is not necessarily captured by an account of what it spends and receives. The government is, directly and indirectly, a major regulating body. Its impact on the economy (and on society in general) can only be fully understood if that side of what it does is recognised. The way it conducts its monetary or exchange-rate policy can have enormous impact on the private sector, and yet not involve a great deal of expenditure or revenue. Even the number of civil servants involved need not be large. The point holds for a policy of exchange control (regulating the international movement of capital), or prices and incomes control. It also holds for policy to promote competition, and regulate monopoly, and for policy to protect the

environment. All of these things require some public expenditure, but their significance is not measured by the scale of
public expenditure. In principle, comparing two governments,
one can have much more impact than the other, and exercise a
greater degree of control of firms and households, even though
it spends and taxes less. (It is useful to distinguish within the
public sector between the central government, local government, and nationalised industries. Within the last of these it is
also worth remarking that the Bank of England is a nationalised industry, although the impression is sometimes created
that it is part of the private sector!)

With that as background let us examine the path of public
expenditure over the past two decades. In Table 8.1 we show a
great deal of the relevant material. The first five columns
show the scale of broadly defined government expenditure.
This is divided between direct expenditure on goods and services and transfer payments, and between current and capital
expenditure.

Perhaps what stands out most of all is the long-run persistent rise in the relative importance of current grants and
transfers. These include such things as unemployment pay,
supplementary benefit, and old age pensions. They represented
about 29% of total government expenditure twenty years ago
and have now risen to 39%. The rise is partly due to the increase
in the number of people requiring help, for example, a growing
fraction of old people in the population, or a drastic rise in the
scale of unemployment. It is also due to a policy shift favouring
this kind of payment. Thus, old age pensions rose by 40%
compared with average incomes,in the 1970s. In the early
eighties, the average transfer payment has not risen as rapidly
as the average income of those in work.

Transfer payments at the time they are made comprise a
transfer from the economically active to the dependent population. Since, however, everyone starts off dependent and almost
everyone eventually becomes dependent, these payments can
also be interpreted as transfers from one period of a person's
life to other periods. Since they are paid for out of taxation,
they are also somewhat redistributive from the better off to
the worse off. The UK tax system is mildly progressive in that
the higher your income, the higher is the average tax you pay.

Table 8.1 The Development of Government Expenditure (at current prices)

	Expenditure on Goods & Services (a) Current £m	(b) Capital £m	(c) Current Grants & Subsidies £m	(d) Capital Transfers £m	(e) Total Public Expenditure £m	(a)/(e)	(c)/(e)	(a)+(c)/(e)	Public Expenditure/GDP at Market Prices
1958	3,751	781	1,875	71	6,478	0.58	0.29	0.87	0.28
1959	3,988	824	2,011	71	6,894	0.58	0.29	0.87	0.29
1960	4,224	843	2,156	86	7,309	0.58	0.29	0.87	0.29
1961	4,557	928	2,419	91	7,995	0.57	0.30	0.87	0.29
1962	4,882	1,042	2,610	114	8,648	0.56	0.30	0.86	0.30
1963	5,138	1,120	2,829	122	9,209	0.56	0.31	0.87	0.30
1964	5,466	1,413	2,930	149	9,958	0.55	0.29	0.84	0.30
1965	5,994	1,509	3,344	182	11,029	0.54	0.30	0.84	0.31
1966	6,520	1,705	3,564	189	11,978	0.54	0.30	0.84	0.32
1967	7,213	1,991	4,177	413	13,794	0.52	0.30	0.82	0.34
1968	7,662	2,204	4,752	695	15,313	0.50	0.31	0.81	0.35
1969	7,997	2,286	4,956	842	16,081	0.50	0.31	0.81	0.35
1970	8,991	2,474	5,391	796	17,652	0.51	0.31	0.82	0.35
1971	10,250	2,613	5,924	912	19,699	0.52	0.30	0.82	0.34
1972	11,675	2,768	7,232	820	22,495	0.52	0.32	0.84	0.35
1973	13,372	3,697	8,221	980	26,270	0.51	0.31	0.82	0.36
1974	16,628	4,406	11,200	1,093	33,327	0.50	0.34	0.84	0.40
1975	22,956	5,004	14,332	1,196	43,488	0.53	0.33	0.86	0.41
1976	26,741	5,442	17,044	1,435	50,662	0.53	0.34	0.87	0.40
1977	29,262	4,880	19,515	1,537	55,194	0.53	0.35	0.88	0.38
1978	33,071	4,662	23,235	2,028	62,996	0.52	0.37	0.89	0.38
1979	38,361	5,138	27,461	1,895	72,855	0.53	0.38	0.91	0.37
1980	48,419	5,618	32,610	2,254	88,901	0.54	0.37	0.91	0.39
1981	54,538	4,528	38,647	2,493	100,206	0.54	0.39	0.93	0.40
1982	60,082	4,534	43,465	2,874	110,955	0.54	0.39	0.93	0.40

(This point should not be exaggerated. The *marginal tax rate* is defined as the extra tax you pay for a given rise in income. Some poor people have effectively high marginal tax rates, partly because of the loss of benefits as their incomes rise a little.) Transfer payments are also aimed towards those who are poor and in need. But this should not be exaggerated, especially the progressiveness of the tax system. Most people pay for most of the benefits they receive over their lifetimes.

Various questions are asked about the system of taxation and transfers connected with incentives. In discussing unemployment, we have mentioned the rise in the replacement ratio and its possible effect on job search and average period away from work. High marginal tax rates are said by some to be a disincentive to effort. If, however, people attach great weight to their incomes net of tax, the effect is the other way round. It could be an incentive to effort, because the more you have to pay in tax the more you have to work to get a particular sum after tax. Some so called 'supply side' economists, especially in the USA, argued that cuts in marginal and average rates of taxation would be an enormous stimulus to effort and enterprise: so much so that incomes would rise sufficiently to leave the government's tax revenue unchanged. Experience in that country has shown them to be in error. (The evidence on all this is inconclusive, and it is doubtful whether the tax effect is significant either way.)

It is also argued that there is a connection between direct taxation and inflation. If workers are concerned with incomes after tax, the higher the level of the tax rate, the larger the money wage they will demand. It is said that this was a contributing factor to the money wage explosions of the 1970s. Certainly average tax rates rose from the late 1960s onwards (see below p. 114). A similar point was made about Sir Geoffrey Howe's early budgetary rise in VAT.

Reverting to our main theme, the behaviour of government current expenditure involved a downward trend in its share up to 1975. Up to the end of the 1960s this was not offset by a major rise in transfer payments. Instead, it went hand in hand with a rise in government capital expenditure. This increased from 13% of public expenditure to 19%. In the 1970s, however, there was a remarkable drop in government capital expenditure. In 1980 it represented only 9% of total government expenditure, having fallen in real terms for several years (see Table 8.1).

We have mentioned the ratio of tax revenue to gross domestic product. Table 8.1 also contains figures on the ratio of public expenditure to gross domestic product. (Recall that we have omitted the interest payments that the government has to pay on the national debt, and some nationalised industries' investment.)

Clearly, there has been a rising trend in the ratio of public expenditure to national income. The trend has continued almost uninterrupted from 1958 to 1975. Since then the ratio has fallen a little, but in 1980 it was still above any level reached before 1974 and it continued to rise in 1981 and 1982.

For the most part the trend has been a smooth one. There was, however, a larger than average jump between 1966 and 1967, and an even larger jump between 1973 and 1974. The fall between 1976 and 1977 was also rather precipitate.

The rise in public expenditure can be put into a slightly different perspective. Let us concentrate on expenditure on goods and services, that is, the money the government actually spends, as opposed to what it transfers to others to spend. This rose from 20% of GDP in 1960 to 21% in 1965, to 22% in 1970 and to 27% in 1975. As before, the mid-1970s represent the peak of public expenditure. Since then the fall has been to 24%.

A similar picture emerges from the share of the labour force who are employed in the public sector. This rose steadily from 24% in the early 1960s to 30% in 1976. It has stayed at that figure since. With the relative share of public expenditure falling since 1975, and with national unemployment rising, it is apparent that public money has been used rather more to maintain public employment.

Can anything be discerned from these figures about the role of public expenditure and taxation as short-run policy tools? Elementary multiplier theory says, for example, that falls in private propensities to spend can be offset by cuts in taxation and increases in public expenditure. Given the extent to which these figures are dominated by a strong trend, few lessons can be drawn from them. Although the public expenditure ratio jumped at a couple of periods when output grew rapidly, it is impossible to say from the figures what caused what. Moreover, there are other variations in output that appear to be unconnected with public expenditure and taxation.

What is also interesting in this connection is the public sector borrowing requirement (PSBR). In broad terms, this measures the difference between the overall expenditure of the public sector and its revenue of various kinds. The difference is made up by borrowing either short-term or long-term. (Some of the borrowing may be from UK sources and some from foreign.)

Short-term borrowing in the form of such things as Treasury Bills is likely to increase the reserve assets of the banking system, enabling the banks to increase the money supply. Long-term borrowing involves a commitment for considerable periods of time to pay interest at possibly very high rates. Compared with the flow of savings, the more the government wishes to borrow long term, and the less it enables the money supply to increase, the higher the interest rate that will rule on the open market.

The relative size of the public sector borrowing requirement indicates, albeit imperfectly, the extent of that sector's surplus or deficit (see Table 8.2). For most of the period under review there has been a positive public sector borrowing requirement. The only exception was 1969 following a strongly contractionary budget, and giving rise to the first post-war major increase in unemployment. If the movement in the PSBR ratio is compared with the movement of real GDP (Table 2.1, Chapter 2), it will be seen that the two are hardly correlated at all. In ten years they move in the same direction, and in seven in the opposite direction. In other words, a rise in the rate of PSBR to GDP may or may not occur in a year in which real GDP grows more rapidly.

This lack of connection is not surprising, and should not be taken to imply that public expenditure and taxation have no impact on the economy. The reason is that, in part, public expenditure and taxation are determined by the level of economic activity, as well as being independent causes of it themselves. A rise in public expenditure will raise national income via the multiplier. But a *fall* in national income will

Table 8.2 Tax Revenues and the Public Sector Borrowing Requirement

	Total Tax Revenue £m	Taxes divided by GDP at Market Prices	Public Sector Borrowing Requirement £m	PSBR divided by GDP at Market Prices
1963	9,023	0.30	844	2.8
1964	9,779	0.30	990	3.0
1965	11,014	0.31	1,208	3.4
1966	12,106	0.32	964	2.5
1967	13,522	0.34	1,860	4.6
1968	15,253	0.35	1,295	3.0
1969	17,138	0.37	−445	−1.0
1970	19,133	0.37	4	0.0
1971	20,281	0.35	1,382	2.4
1972	21,461	0.34	2,039	3.2
1973	24,101	0.33	4,198	5.7
1974	30,024	0.36	6,365	7.6
1975	38,521	0.37	10,477	9.9
1976	44,621	0.36	9,144	7.3
1977	50,781	0.35	5,975	4.1
1978	56,425	0.34	8,335	5.0
1979	67,437	0.35	12,638	6.5
1980	82,144	0.36	12,192	5.4
1981	95,382	0.38	10.620	4.2
1982	107,088	0.39	5,432	2.0

cause a rise in such items of public expenditure as unemployment pay and supplementary benefits. It will also cause a fall in tax revenue. Thus, an increase in the *net* expenditure of the public sector may go hand in hand with either a rise or fall in national income. It depends on what is causing what at the time. Thus, it would be strange if anything very clear-cut emerged from the sort of rough examination of the data we have been engaged in. It is also important to remember that a given increase in public expenditure does not have the same effect as a decrease in taxation of the same size. Some of the latter may be at the expense of private saving. Moreover, the import content of private spending may differ from that of public spending. This reinforces the point that it is the whole structure of the budget that needs to be examined, and not just the PSBR.

Let us now look at the growth of public expenditure in real terms. In Table 8.3 are shown general government final (or consumption) expenditure on goods and services together with gross domestic capital formation by general government. The sum of the two are also shown. These are all in real terms, that is at 1980 prices.

Government current expenditure on goods and services shows a continuous upward trend. It has grown by an average of 2.2% per annum in the period, being about 50% higher in 1980 than in 1962. It has, however, fluctuated pretty considerably in the period. In two years, 1967 and 1975, it grew very rapidly, indeed at more than 2½ times its average annual rate. In three other years, 1969, 1977 and 1981, it actually fell. That latter consideration is obviously pretty rare, occurring only three times in twenty-one years. It may, however, become common in future. (It is worth remarking that in the previous decade, general government final consumption fell in four successive years between 1954 and 1958.) It looks as if any sustained burst in this form of government spending is eventually stopped and reversed, possibly because of economic crisis. There was devaluation late in 1967 followed by strong deflation of the economy, a steep rise in unemployment and an eventual balance of payments surplus. In 1976 there was another economic crisis, recourse to borrowing from the International Monetary Fund, another steep rise in unemployment, and an eventual reduction in the inflation rate.

The capital side is more remarkable. Over the whole period general government annual real expenditure on capital projects has actually declined. It was 12% lower in 1980 than in 1962 and there was a further massive decline in 1981. Its history seems to be divided into four parts; (a) very rapid expansion in the 1960s, (b) a subsequent pause with modest decline, (c) a massive boost in 1973, (d) continuous and considerable decline since 1973. What is also noteworthy is how much the level of government capital spending has jumped about. In Chapter 3 the question was raised whether public

Table 8.3 Government Expenditure and Capital Formation at 1980 Prices, £m

	Government Expenditure on Goods and Services (Consumption) (a)	Percentage Change	General Government Gross Domestic Fixed Capital Formation (b)	Percentage Change	(a) + (b)	Percentage Change
1962	33,175		6,492		39,667	
1963	33,714	1.6	6,514	0.3	40,228	1.4
1964	34,252	1.6	7,932	21.8	42,184	4.9
1965	35,161	2.7	8,208	3.5	43,369	2.8
1966	36,093	2.7	8,822	7.5	44,915	3.6
1967	38,151	5.7	10,140	14.9	48,291	7.6
1968	38,294	0.4	10,647	5.0	48,941	1.4
1969	37,582	−1.9	10,464	−1.7	48,046	−1.8
1970	38,129	1.5	10,639	1.7	48,768	1.5
1971	39,266	3.0	10,293	−3.3	49,559	1.6
1972	40,885	4.1	9,864	−4.2	50,749	2.4
1973	42,814	4.7	11,041	11.9	53,855	6.1
1974	43,465	1.5	10,294	−6.8	53,759	−0.2
1975	45,814	5.4	9,444	−8.3	55,258	2.8
1976	46,249	0.9	9,169	−3.0	55,418	0.3
1977	45,734	−1.1	7,684	−16.2	53,418	−3.6
1978	46,730	2.2	6,787	−11.7	53,517	0.2
1979	47,612	1.9	6,446	−5.0	54,058	1.0
1980	48,419	1.7	5,618	−12.8	54,037	0.0
1981	48,329	−0.2	4,015	−28.5	52,344	−3.1
1982	49,011	1.4	3,938	−1.9	52,949	1.2

sector spending was stabilising or destabilising. If it has a high variance, this is still compatible with its being an offset to other highly variable expenditure. Whatever view is taken of that, it is apparent that those parts of the private sector specifically devoted to public sector capital projects must have found it hard to cope with the variability. In addition, the decline in annual expenditure of about 50% since 1974 can hardly have been conducive to profitability.

This evidence shows fairly conclusively that it is unlikely that excessive government capital expenditure can have crowded out private capital expenditure in the second half of the 1970s and early part of the 1980s. More generally, if the total of current and capital expenditure is examined, it will be seen that this grew at an average rate of 1.8% per annum. This is distinctly below the underlying growth rate of gross domestic product (see Chapter 2).

Total real expenditure is plotted in Figure 8.1. It has an upward trend, but one which is tailing off. There is a rapid rise ending in about 1973. After that there is little overall expansion. The boost in 1967 is distinctly above trend, as is the decline in 1969. This fluctuation is interesting because, as we have remarked, it is associated with economic crisis. After 1973, however, we seem to enter an entirely new era with no net expansion. Since a great deal of the expenditure we are talking about consists of purchases from the private sector, it is not surprising that a degree of stagnation has persisted in this period. Apparently, restraint on public expenditure of this kind has created room for a degree of expansion of private expenditure which has not occurred. Elementary macro-economic theory would predict a relatively low level of GDP and rising unemployment in these circumstances. Paradoxically, more sophisticated and rather anti-Keynesian theory led to more optimistic views which were not borne out in the period under discussion. (This does not mean that they would be erroneous in other circumstances.)

Since figures for general government final expenditure are published in both current and constant prices, it is possible to calculate an implied price index by dividing the latter into the former. This is an index of the prices of goods and services bought by the general government sector. It is of interest to

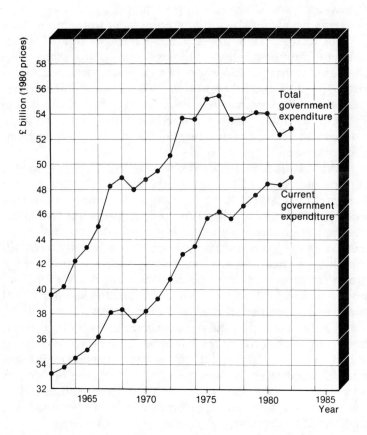

Figure 8.1

compare its behaviour with the general level of prices, and it will be recalled that we did this in discussing inflation in Chapter 5. We showed there that there was a kind of relative price effect, the average prices of goods bought by the government increasing relative to prices in general.

Finally, we look again at employment in the public and private sectors. Table 8.4 gives the relevant figures. What emerges from these is that, if the size of the public sector were measured in terms of its share of total employment, this has risen from 24% in 1961 to 30% in 1980. In employment terms, the public sector appears relatively less significant than it does in tax or expenditure terms. Nonetheless, the broad picture of a rise in the public sector reaching a peak in 1975 remains about the same.

What is also apparent from the employment figures is the considerable rise in local authority activity. The fraction of the employed labour force working in local authorities rose from 7.6% to 12.3%, the absolute increase being 1,157,000. This is a large share of the decline in private sector employment. Central government employment has risen by over half a million. Public corporation employment has fluctuated a great deal (largely as a result of nationalisation, denationalisation, renationalisation and so on), but is a little less significant at the end of the period than at the beginning.

To the extent that the private sector and public corporations provide the economic basis on which central government and local authorities stand, their task has in a simple sense got more difficult over the two decades. In fact, the problem is understated because the private sector and nationalised industries also have to generate incomes which can be taxed and transferred to the growing number of unemployed.

Nonetheless, it cannot be inferred from these data that the cause of the UK's economic difficulties was the growth of local authority and central government employment. It may have been, but was not necessarily so. It is possible that, if public sector employment were lower, private sector employment would have been higher, that is, that the local authorities and central government crowded out the private sector. But it is also possible that, if employment were lower in the public sector, most of these people would simply have been unem-

Table 8.4 Employment in the Public and Private Sectors

	Central Government		Local Authority		Public Corporations		Private Sector		Total
	'000	%	'000	%	'000	%	'000	%	'000
1961	1,773	7.2	1,870	7.6	2,200	9.0	18,614	76.1	24,457
1962	1,768	7.2	1,940	7.9	2,196	8.9	18,728	76.0	24,632
1963	1,770	7.2	2,008	8.1	2,136	8.7	18,747	76.0	24,661
1964	1,771	7.1	2,088	8.4	2,079	8.3	19,012	76.2	24,950
1965	1,793	7.1	2,154	8.5	2,025	8.0	19,231	76.3	25,203
1966	1,819	7.2	2,259	8.9	1,962	7.7	19,315	76.2	25,355
1967	1,872	7.5	2,364	9.5	2,164	8.7	18,592	74.4	24,992
1968	1,885	7.6	2,444	9.8	2,069	8.3	18,443	74.2	24,841
1969	1,864	7.5	2,505	10.1	2,041	8.2	18,447	74.2	24,857
1970	1,905	7.7	2,559	10.3	2,025	8.2	18,264	73.8	24,753
1971	1,940	8.0	2,651	10.9	2,009	8.2	17,799	72.9	24,399
1972	1,979	8.1	2,771	11.3	1,929	7.9	17,810	72.7	24,489
1973	1,998	8.0	2,890	11.5	1,890	7.5	18,279	72.9	25,057
1974	2,096	8.3	2,834	11.3	1,985	7.9	18,215	72.5	25,130
1975	2,251	9.0	2,974	11.9	2,035	8.1	17,780	71.0	25,040
1976	2,314	9.3	3,016	12.1	1,980	8.0	17,518	70.6	24,828
1977	2,305	9.3	2,984	12.0	2,089	8.4	17,472	70.3	24,850
1978	2,307	9.2	2,997	12.0	2,061	8.2	17,634	70.5	24,999
1979	2,319	9.2	3,060	12.1	2,065	8.2	17,874	70.6	25,318
1980	2,327	9.2	3,027	12.0	2,036	8.1	17,801	70.7	25,193
1981	2,359	9.8	2,966	12.3	1,867	7.7	16,961	70.2	24,153
1982	2,346	9.9	2,931	12.3	1,759	7.4	16,729	70.4	23,765

ployed. With less spending power, their effective demand would also have been lower. Thus, private sector output and employment would also have been diminished.

Questions

1. What evidence would you examine to determine the incentive (or disincentive) effects of taxation? How would you expect different types of households and firms to be affected by taxation?

2. Can there be incentive effects of public expenditure?

3. Our definition of public expenditure is not as broad as it might be. Examine how the ratio of public expenditure to national income increases if all nationalised industry investment and interest on the national debt are included.

4. A rise in national income will cause a rise in all forms of tax revenue. Do you think this will encourage the government to spend more? How might such a relationship make more difficult any attempt to estimate the government expenditure multiplier?

5. Why do you think real government capital spending has declined so drastically since 1973? What sort of forces might cause this trend to be reversed?

6. We have referred here and in Chapter 5 to the relative price effect. Would you expect it to be as significant for government capital expenditure as for current expenditure?

9
Growth

It is customary in economics to distinguish short-run changes in output from long-run trends. The subject of economic growth concerns the way these long-run trends are determined. (As a curiosity, when the discussion is about the poorer countries of the world, as opposed to the advanced industrialised ones, the expression used is 'economic development'.)

The growth rate (or the 'underlying' growth rate) of a country is the annual percentage increase in its real gross domestic product measured over a long period of time, that is, decades rather than two or three years. In shorter periods of time, output varies as the degree of utilisation of available resources changes. A fall in output may cause some machinery to be used less intensively or not at all, while members of the labour force may work fewer hours or become wholly unemployed. Similarly, a rise in output may cause machines and men to be used more intensively, and the unemployed to be brought into work again. These variations in output associated with deviations from the norm in resource utilisation are the cyclical ones.

Over time, however, there will be more persistent changes. Some of these are quantitative. Capital investment implies an increase in the availability of inanimate resources such as machines, factories, roads, and so on. Clearly, they raise the productive potential of the economy. Similarly, long-run trends in the size of the labour force, or the average hours which men and women wish to work, also represent a resource change which affects productive potential.

In addition to these quantitative changes, there are more

123

qualitative ones to be taken into account. Existing technical knowhow may be used more or less effectively. The more efficiently machines and workers combine, the larger the resulting flow of output. This may be regarded as partly a matter of good as opposed to poor management. But British experience suggests that it is more than that. It appears that we in this country do not use available methods to anything like their full potential, and the causes of our failure to do so lie very deep in the structure of our society.

A second qualitative factor is the improvement in technology. New kinds of machinery are invented, new processes are discovered, and existing ones are modified and made to operate better. New capital equipment, whether it merely replaces existing or worn-out equipment or is a new addition to it, is superior to what existed before.

Thirdly, there is the improvement in the quality of the labour force. Education and training may make the existing labour force more productive. New entrants to the labour force, especially when they have gained some work experience, may be more up to date and better trained than those who retire.

All these quantitative and qualitative forces will determine the level of output which is obtained from existing resources, and the rate at which that output grows. It should be added, to extend a point just alluded to, that these are all economic in character, but underlying them are the institutions of economy and society. Attitudes to work, to mobility, responsiveness to change, willingness to innovate and take risks, all help to determine economic performance, and the causes of these lie to a large extent outside economics. More to the point, while they may be recognised, it cannot be said yet that social scientists are at all close to a full understanding of them.

Let us now turn to the examination of the growth experience of the UK economy. Since we wish to concentrate on changes in output not due to changes in resource use, our measurement must meet two criteria:

(i)   The years compared must lie sufficiently far apart to correspond to the longer run.

(ii) The degree of resource utilisation must be comparable.

The first point is obvious. On the second, what we are trying to avoid is biasing our calculation by, for example, choosing the start year as one of full employment and the end year as one of large scale unemployment. Output in the latter will be abnormally low so that the estimate of the growth rate will itself be biased downwards. If, however, the gap between the two years is very large, this bias may not matter too much. Thus, output in the end year may be 5% below normal. In a twenty-year calculation of growth, this will bias the estimate downwards by about 0.25%, that is, a country whose true growth rate was 3% per annum would appear to have a growth rate of 2.75% per annum. The difference in this simple case is not trivial but it is not overwhelming. More generally, as we shall see, the problem it arises from *is* of considerable importance to the UK.

In chapter 2 we have already seen that in the 23 years from 1959 to 1982 gross domestic product at constant factor cost grew by two thirds, that is, 67%. This represents a growth rate of 2.3% per annum throughout the period. Comparing the first half of the period with the second, the relevant growth rates were 3.1% per annum and 1.5% per annum.

Is it really true that the underlying growth rate of the UK economy halved between 1959 and 1982? One way of answering this is to consider whether the degree of resource utilisation was the same at the beginning of the period as at the end. It has already been shown that, according to at least one measure, it was not. How are we to get round this?

One way would be to take account of changes in the employed labour force. In 1959 this was approximately 24 million, in 1969 it was 25 million, and in 1982, 23.8 million. The growth rate of GDP per member of the employed labour force was 3.0% per annum in the earlier period and still 1.87% in the later one. Thus, the margin is lowered but a significant gap remains.

Another possible approach is to adjust output by the change in the unemployment percentage. This was 2.1% in 1959, 2.4% in 1969, 2.6% in 1970, and 12.7% in 1982. The difference between the first three is minute. It is the fourth that creates the problems. Suppose, to allow for it, output in 1982 were adjudged to be (say) 7.5% below full capacity. This would imply that the growth rate in the second period was 2.4% per annum. This still implies a fall in the growth rate of the UK economy, but not as large a one as the earlier calculations had indicated.

If the underlying growth rate of the UK economy has fallen in the 1970s and early 1980s, compared with the 1960s, why is this so? Nobody is at all sure, and, therefore, needless to say, there are countless possible explanations. In the 1960s, the working population (that is, the number of people available for work) grew by 2%, whereas in the 1970s it grew by 5%, hardly an enormous difference. The employed labour force grew by 2% in the earlier decade and has fallen by 5% in the past dozen years.

The next possibility is average hours worked. This fell by about 3% in each decade, so that too hardly explains very much. (There has been about a 3% drop in average hours worked in manufacturing in the early 1980s.) On capital accumulation, we have already shown that it did not fall much relative to GDP in the 1970s, and that the share of private sector investment within the overall total increased. Private sector investment fell in 1974 and 1975, but then rose again and by 1977 was back to its earlier levels. It started to fall again in 1980 and 1981, but recovered in 1982. It is, therefore, not easy to see that as being of overwhelming significance.

There are two other explanations that may be considered. One concerns the relative decline of the manufacturing sector and the other the effect of the rise in the price of oil. The two are, of course, interrelated.

Before analysing them we shall look at another related concept, *national disposable income*. The importance of this arises from international trade. We may define the terms of trade as the price of our exports relative to our imports. The terms of trade tell us how much we have to export for a given volume of imports. The less we have to export to pay for our imports, the more of our own output we can keep for ourselves, and the better off we are. A consequence of the OPEC price rise of 1973 was that we had to give the oil producers more of our output to pay for whatever oil we wished to import. The terms of trade moved against us or became adverse. Gross domestic product as it is usually calculated does not take this effect into account; national disposable income does. The growth rate of national disposable income in the 1960s was 3.1% per annum, about the same as the growth rate of GDP. In the 1970s, national disposable income grew by 1.5% per annum rather than the 1.6% per annum of GDP. Within the 1970s, what is most important to note is the period after 1973. From 1973 to 1977 real GDP grew by 2.3%, whereas national disposable income fell by 1.7%. Since then, because the UK has North Sea oil, the position has changed. A rise in the price of oil no longer necessarily worsens our terms of trade, and national disposable income has grown more rapidly than domestic product at constant factor cost. Between 1977 and 1982, GDP has gone up by 2.9% while national disposable income has gone up 7.6%.

From 1959 to 1973, real GDP grew at a rate of 3.1% per annum. Since then, the growth rate has been half that. This suggests that the original oil price rise has something to do with the decline in the growth rate. This may have happened in a number of ways.

The most obvious is that the rise in the price of oil will cause some kinds of existing equipment and processes which use a great deal of energy to become obsolete. (To the extent that the oil price rise causes demand to switch to alternative energy sources, the prices of these rise too.) This obsolescence is of an economic kind. Equipment is used if it is profitable to do so. Higher energy costs may be partly offset by a relative fall in the costs of other productive equipment and also by a rise in the price of the final product. But energy-intensive machinery will suffer compared with that using less energy, causing its use no longer to be justified. Thus, the rise in the price of energy is akin to the destruction of some of the existing capital stock.

One of the consequences of oil cost push has been stagflation. If real output is depressed and costs are high, profits will be low. These factors may depress investment directly, and also because they make businessmen pessimistic about future prospects. Low growth now, by reducing the rate of capital accumulation and inhibiting innovation, will cause low growth in the future. There may be some truth in this argument, but we have already pointed out that, although private sector investment fell immediately following the 1973 oil price rise, not long after that it picked up again and in 1982 was 37% above its level of 1970.

It would be wrong, however, to take this interpretation at its face value. At the one extreme, investment in petroleum and natural gas rose from £410m. per annum in 1972 to £2,778m. in 1982 (both at 1980 prices). There is the point made earlier that the oil price rise has rendered a good deal of capital obsolete from the economic point of view. More of the existing investment is needed to replace this and is not, therefore, a net addition to the capital stock. Compared with these, investment in manufacturing fell from £6,344m. per annum to £4,457m. The path of the latter is most interesting and is plotted in Figure 9.1. The percentage change in manufacturing investment is in Table 9.1. It has a pronounced cyclical movement, and shows a remarkable recovery after 1976. It has fallen in three successive years, starting in 1980, and is now 40% below its peak of 1979. (It should be emphasised that the falls in 1971 and 1972 were more precipitate than those of the later period, and they antedate OPEC.)

Manufacturing industry is thought to be extremely important for economic growth because of its potential for innovation and improvements in productivity. (This should not, of course, be taken to mean that productivity improvements cannot occur in other sectors, including those which provide services rather than goods, especially if the output of those sectors is measured correctly.) It is worth looking, therefore, at what has been happening to manufacturing production and employment in recent years.

In Table 9.2 we show the indexes of manufacturing output, and of total industrial production. They move in a similar fashion up to 1975. After that it is apparent that industrial production as a whole relies to a greater extent on oil and gas. Therefore, it gives a greater impression of buoyancy than does the series for manufacturing output alone.

In Table 9.3 the figures for the percentage change in the series are given and these are plotted in Figures 9.2 and 9.3. What is immediately apparent from that information is that the manufacturing sector was growing at a steady rate up to 1973, but after 1973 its growth rate drops significantly, and

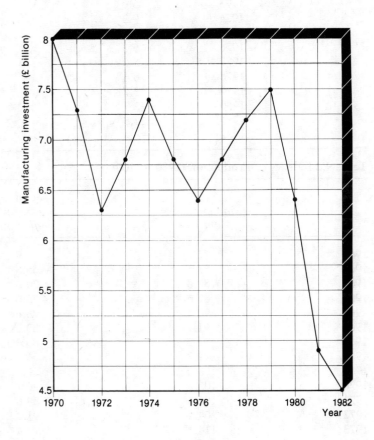

Figure 9.1

Table 9.1 Percentage Change in Manufacturing Industry
Investment (1980 prices)

1972	7.8
1973	6.6
1974	9.3
1975	−8.3
1976	−5.1
1977	5.0
1978	6.6
1979	3.7
1980	−13.7
1981	−24.5
1982	−8.4

Table 9.2 Indexes of Production (1980 = 100)

	Manufacturing Output	Total Industrial Production
1961	77.3	67.9
1962	77.5	68.5
1963	80.3	70.8
1964	87.6	76.6
1965	90.1	78.8
1966	91.7	80.0
1967	92.2	80.6
1968	99.3	86.7
1969	103.0	89.7
1970	103.3	90.1
1971	102.3	89.6
1972	104.4	91.2
1973	114.1	99.4
1974	112.7	97.4
1975	104.9	92.2
1976	106.9	95.2
1977	108.9	100.1
1978	109.6	103.1
1979	109.5	107.1
1980	100.0	100.0
1981	93.1	95.9
1982	92.4	97.1

Table 9.3 Annual Percentage Change in Production

	Manufacturing Output	Total Industrial Production
1962	0.3	0.9
1963	3.6	3.4
1964	9.1	8.2
1965	2.9	2.9
1966	1.8	1.5
1967	0.5	0.8
1968	7.7	7.6
1969	3.7	3.5
1970	0.3	0.4
1971	−1.0	−0.6
1972	2.1	1.8
1973	9.3	9.0
1974	−1.2	−2.0
1975	−6.9	−5.3
1976	1.9	3.3
1977	1.9	5.1
1978	0.6	3.0
1979	−0.1	3.9
1980	−8.7	−6.6
1981	−6.9	−4.1
1982	−0.8	1.3

over the whole of these seven years becomes negative. Indeed, up to 1973 manufacturing industry grew at an average annual rate of 3.4%. From 1974 onwards it *declined* at an average annual rate of 2.2%.

Turning to the numbers employed in manufacturing, the figures are shown in Table 9.4 and plotted in Figures 9.4 and 9.5. Employment in manufacturing was fairly steady up to 1966. In 1967 it starts to decline, with strong falls occurring in 1971 and 1972, 1975 and 1976, and 1980–82. Altogether, from 1967 onwards the decline is pretty definite.

Labour productivity in manufacturing may be defined as the ratio of manufacturing output to the number of people employed in manufacturing. The level and rate of change of productivity are shown in Table 9.5 and Figures 9.6 and 9.7.

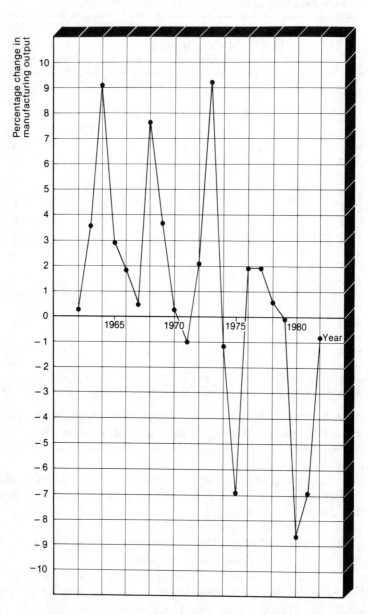

Figure 9.2

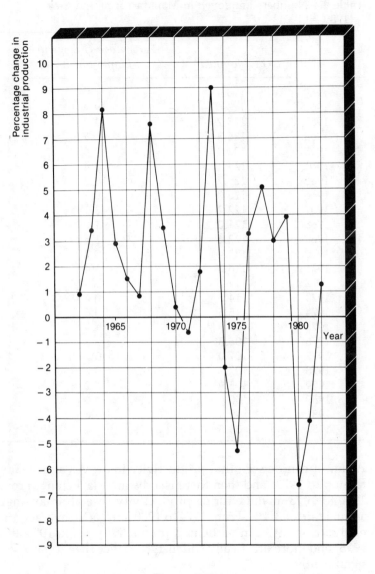

Figure 9.3

Table 9.4 Numbers Employed in Manufacturing Industry
(1980 = 100)

	Employment	Percentage Change in Employment
1959	118.4	
1960	123.6	4.4
1961	125.2	1.2
1962	124.3	−0.7
1963	122.3	−1.6
1964	124.1	1.4
1965	125.7	1.3
1966	126.0	0.3
1967	122.2	−3.1
1968	121.0	−1.0
1969	122.6	1.4
1970	122.4	−0.2
1971	118.2	−3.4
1972	114.2	−3.4
1973	114.8	0.6
1974	115.5	0.6
1975	109.9	−4.9
1976	106.3	−3.3
1977	107.0	0.7
1978	107.2	0.2
1979	105.9	−1.2
1980	100.0	−5.6
1981	90.4	−9.6
1982	85.5	−5.4

Again, it can be seen that productivity improves at a steady rate up to 1973, and then there is a distinct slackening. From 1960 to 1973 manufacturing productivity rose at an average annual rate of 3.4%. From 1974 to 1980 it fell at an average annual rate of 1.9%. In particular, productivity fell in 1974 and 1975, and more drastically still in 1980. Since then it has risen significantly.

It might be argued that instead of measuring productivity by output per person employed, we ought to measure it by output per person hour. The relevant figures are given in Table 9.6.

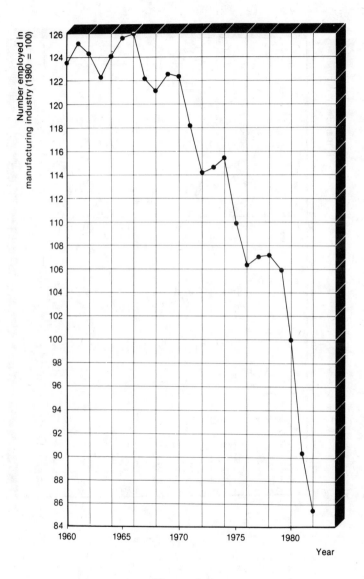

Figure 9.4

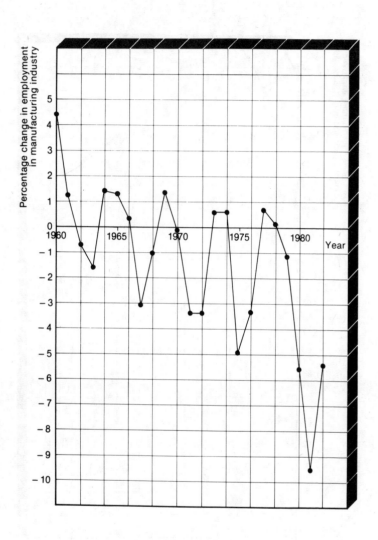

Figure 9.5

Table 9.5 Manufacturing Productivity (1980 = 100)

	Productivity	Percentage Change in Productivity
1959	61	
1960	63	3.5
1961	63	−1.1
1962	63	1.0
1963	66	5.2
1964	71	7.6
1965	72	1.5
1966	73	1.6
1967	76	3.7
1968	82	8.2
1969	84	2.4
1970	84	0.0
1971	86	2.4
1972	91	5.8
1973	99	8.8
1974	97	−2.0
1975	95	−2.1
1976	100	5.3
1977	101	1.0
1978	102	1.0
1979	103	1.0
1980	100	−3.0
1981	103	3.0
1982	110	7.0

As can be seen, this measure, while not exactly the same as the previous one, gives very nearly the same picture of events. Either way, productivity was higher in 1982 than at any earlier time in manufacturing. But the increase in productivity was no greater in 1981 and 1982 than in some earlier years such as 1976, or 1972 and 1973.

Overall, the deteriorating economic performance of the UK economy is confirmed. Moreover, examination of manufacturing reinforces the view that the 1973 oil price rise was an important contributing factor. Nonetheless, there are

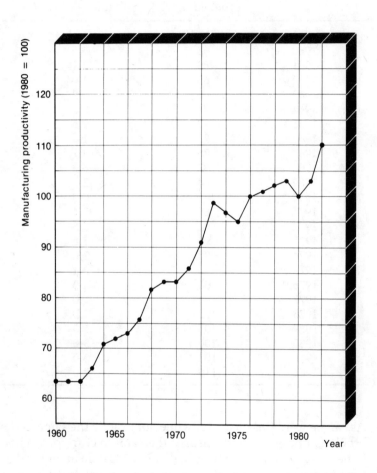

Figure 9.6

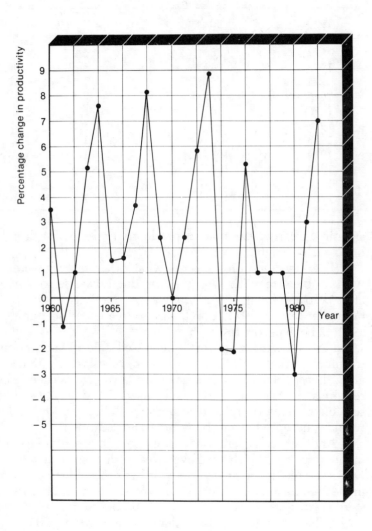

Figure 9.7

Table 9.6 Output per person hour in manufacturing

	Level (1980 = 100)	Percentage Change
1970	80	
1971	83	3.8
1972	88	6.0
1973	94	6.8
1974	95	1.1
1975	93	−2.1
1976	98	5.4
1977	99	1.0
1978	100	1.0
1979	101	1.0
1980	100	−1.0
1981	105	5.0
1982	110	5.0

signs in the early 1980s that the productivity trends of a decade or so earlier might be returned to.

The key question concerns what other factors were at work in the late 1970s. Why did productivity rise so slowly after 1976 and fall in 1980? Why was productivity in that year no higher than in 1973? Can the improvements discernible in 1981–2 be expected to continue?

Part of the answer lies in the depressed state of the economy for much of that period. In a recession, firms do not immediately divest themselves of labour not currently needed. The reason is that they believe it will be needed in due course. It is sensible to hang on to staff (especially skilled workers) who would otherwise have to be rehired and retrained.

Another consideration relates to the profitability of manufacturing, which we have already discussed. If money wages rise relative to prices, it will be less profitable to produce in the manufacturing sector. Moreover, if the external value of sterling rises, it will be harder to sell abroad, which reinforces the decline in manufacturing. Again as long as that is thought to be temporary, output will fall more than employment, causing productivity to fall.

The rise in the exchange rate will be partly the result of an improved balance of payments, a state of affairs which is expected to continue for some time. A surplus on current account may be attributable to North Sea oil, that is, a lower propensity to import oil and a greater propensity to export it. We then have a paradox. The initial oil price rise damaged the industrial base of the country by raising the price of energy. A later oil price rise coupled with North Sea oil damaged the industrial base by raising the value of sterling and making it harder to export!

In 1982 the country started to move out of recession. The exchange rate has been devalued, and wage inflation has diminished. In addition, there has been a restoration of profits. All these factors imply the end of the worsening of the depression, but it is impossible to say whether they herald a new era of continuous and fast expansion.

Questions

1. Why is UK management unable to use available methods to their full potential? Given your explanation, what evidence would you examine to decide whether or not it was true?

2. How would you test whether education is a productive process? Would you expect all education to make the labour force more efficient?

3. Can you think of a direct way of measuring the economy's capacity to produce (and, therefore, give a more exact estimate of spare capacity at any time)?

4. Would you agree that the main problem with the oil price explosion of 1973 was its unexpected character? Could it have been forecast? What about the later rise of 1978?

5. In a depression, productivity may appear to fall because some workers are kept on in expectation of an upswing. If employers become more pessimistic, and cease to believe in the upswing, they will in due course lay their workers off. Productivity will then appear to rise. What do you conclude about the care that needs to be taken in assessing changes in productivity trends?

10
Some Conclusions

In this last chapter we concern ourselves with a brief discussion of the key problems of the UK economy as they exist today. Essentially, the picture that emerges up to 1973 is of an economy which was rather stable, had a controllable inflation rate, fairly low unemployment, and a moderate rate of real growth. There then appears to be a serious break in which economic performance along every dimension deteriorates. (The sole exception is the current account towards the end of the period, but that is due solely to North Sea oil.) From 1979 onwards, there were important policy changes which led initially to a worsening of the inflation rate and a decline in output. Since then, the inflation rate has diminished and output has recovered. By the end of 1983, however, output was still below its 1979 level.

We have noted that the worsening of the inflation rate occurred at about the same time for other advanced industrialised countries. In Table 10.1 we show that a similar deterioration occurred in unemployment. Whatever the causes of what has gone wrong, some of them must have been common to all countries. Of those there are three obvious ones to bear in mind. Nearly all countries suffered from the moderate rise in inflation in the late 1960s. They were all affected by the ending of the Bretton Woods system of fixed exchange rates, and they were all affected by OPEC.

It could be argued that these forces were sufficient to create worldwide inflation and a strong anti-inflationary reaction by governments. Contractionary policies were introduced to deal with inflation. These lowered output and employment and damaged the market optimism on which sustained growth

Table 10.1 Average Unemployment Percentage, European Countries

	1950−60	1961−72	1973−82
Austria	3.3	1.8	2.0
Belgium	3.2	2.1	7.2
France	1.1	1.8	5.1
W. Germany	2.3	1.1	4.6
Italy	5.5	4.4	7.0
Netherlands	1.7	1.2	4.8
Norway	1.4	1.6	2.0
Sweden	1.8	1.8	2.2
UK	1.7	2.4	6.4

depends. Stagflation may have been the inevitable consequence of higher inflation, but it could be that government policy exacerbated matters.

As far as the UK is concerned, there are two additional considerations to bring to mind. One is that, as we have shown, some trend of higher inflation and unemployment significantly antedates 1973. The second is that the deterioration of our economic performance since then has been worse than the average for our competitors. It is nearly impossible to find a country that appears to have mismanaged its affairs in the past ten years to the degree that the UK has. (Perhaps, it should be added, to avoid accusations of bias, that the period was divided about equally by the two major parties in government.) But it should be added that there was a recovery in 1982−3 which preceded that of the rest of the EEC.

It is apparent that the UK found it much harder to control its inflation. Excessive rises in nominal incomes at the beginning, and powerful cost push throughout the period are to blame. The result has been tougher contractionary policies by government, causing unemployment. This was true both in the middle 1970s and in the early 1980s. A rising exchange rate towards the end of the period also did not help.

What then is the economic outlook? What does elementary macroeconomic theory suggest about policy?

If there is unemployment, the simplest textbook suggestion is that the government must do something to raise effective demand. Government expenditure may be raised or taxation reduced, and effective demand and output will rise via a multiplier process. The additional government expenditure may be on current goods and services, on capital, on the employment of more people in the public sector, or on transfer payments to households or firms. The reduction in taxation may also be divided between households and firms. There will thus be a problem in deciding whether the extra expenditure should occur largely in the private or public sectors, and the extent to which it should stimulate capital as opposed to current spending.

The central point, the need to raise spending, remains. If, however, the focus is on inflation, the opposite appears to be the case. The elementary response to rising prices would be to dampen down demand. The reduction in expenditure would make all markets less buoyant, and cause inflation to diminish, if not to disappear altogether.

For the past few years we have had inflation and unemployment. It seems to be the case, therefore, that we are in a policy dilemma. Stagflation seems to call simultaneously for both a rise and a fall in demand.

Moreover, the dilemma remains if monetary policy is considered. A reduction in interest rates and an easing of the money supply may raise effective demand to some degree, but may also make it more likely that the inflationary process will be intensified.

It should not be forgotten that fiscal and monetary policy are interrelated. An increase in public expenditure or a cut in taxation will initially tend to raise the government's budget deficit. If the government borrows long-term to finance this, interest rates may rise, and some private expenditure (that part sensitive to higher interest rates) will fall. Short-term government borrowing, at the other extreme, adds to the money supply, in that it provides reserve assets for the commercial banks. The result might again be seen to be more inflation.

The true pessimist will see matters as worse still. He will have noted that in some sectors, costs are too high relative to prices and productivity. They will not find it profitable to respond to a demand expansion even if it occurs. In other sectors the view will be taken that rising demand will cause workers to ask for more money wages, and their own suppliers' prices to rise. Thus, they too will respond more by increasing prices rather than output.

If there are supply constraints of this sort, an increase in demand will not help to solve the output and employment problem. It will worsen the inflation problem. Furthermore, with UK firms unwilling to respond, demand will transfer itself to foreign suppliers. Imports will rise and the balance of trade deteriorate. A floating pound will tend to sink, causing import prices in sterling terms to rise, and adding one more twist to the inflation spiral.

On capital account, if interest rates are kept low, and inflation is expected to get worse, funds will flow out, intensifying the downward pressure on the exchange rate. Alternatively, the need to prevent this means that UK interest rates cannot diverge far from those set abroad, notably in New York. In that case high US rates of interest may inhibit expansionary policies here.

Is there any way of dissipating the gloom? Are we doomed to permanent stagflation, our only choice being between even more unemployment or higher inflation?

If we re-examine the argument, the crux of the matter lies in two areas. On the one hand, there is the proposition that inflation will get worse as long as markets become more buoyant. Another way of putting this is to say that it is only spare capacity and unemployment that cause firms to moderate price increases and workers' wage increases. On the other hand, there are supply constraints in the sense of it not being profitable to expand output. (Incidentally, as time goes by there may also be supply constraints in a more ordinary sense. Low levels of investment and little industrial training may reduce the physical capacity to produce.) As economic theory tells us, therefore, both demand and supply side policies are needed.

Expansion would work, therefore, if costs did not rise relative to prices. That would deal with the profitability problem. Inflation would not rise if that was achieved by costs rising relatively more slowly, rather than prices relatively more quickly. Both effects would be achieved to a greater degree and more quickly, if the policies were believed in and expected to work.

Economists have suggested three ways of enabling real expansion to occur without intensifying the pressure on prices. One is to argue by way of expectations. If effective demand in money terms is set to rise at a given rate, it will be apparent to employers and employees that too great a rise in prices and wages can only lead to more unemployment. Thus, they will respond rationally by reducing the inflationary pressure they exert. Gradually, nominal demand can be stepped down, easing the rate of rise of prices and wages, while allowing output and employment to increase.

All that can be said about this approach is that, if it works at all, it takes a very long time. Demand restraint certainly causes unemployment. It is not obvious that people's long-term expectations change as a result, or that real inflationary pressure is ultimately reduced. The fall in inflation in the early 1980s has clearly been connected with the rise in unemployment. The extent to which the fall is permanent is a moot point and, therefore, so too is the extent to which expectations of a non-inflationary kind are prevalent in the economy.

A second view is to devise a series of tax and subsidy policies which penalise those who raise prices and wages too rapidly and help those who show restraint. This approach has not been tested. It has the obvious difficulty of being potentially rather bureaucratic. It may penalise efficient firms who are forced for other reasons to meet a wage demand and raise prices. There is also the question of whether such a policy could be used in the public sector, especially to cope with wage pressures from groups of employees with considerable monopoly power.

These problems of arbitrariness also arise with the third approach of a detailed prices and incomes policy. That involves the setting of norms, coupled with a procedure for allowing deviations from them. In the past such policies have helped temporarily to solve the inflation problem. The unanswered question is whether they are sustainable in the longer run.

It may be said of all three policies that they are not without difficulties. Apart from anything else, in a parliamentary democracy each will be subject to considerable political pressure. It is always tempting for the opposition to undermine what the government is trying to do, by promising better times ahead.

One conclusion may be to combine all three approaches. Demand could be expanded at a given rate, and the government could commit itself to continual expansion, and encouragement of growth and higher productivity. Secondly, it could commit itself to not providing funds to finance continuing high rates of inflation. Instead, it would tax excessive wage increases, and subsidise firms able to negotiate lower wages and set lower prices. Thirdly, there would be a new prices and incomes commission to deal with the inevitable appearance of special cases.

To revert to the textbooks, however, none of this detracts from the simple theoretical point. Rising output requires demand to increase relative to supply. Reduced inflation requires the prices at which output is supplied to fall relative to the prices demanders are offering. The two together would mean the end of stagflation.

Appendix I

The most elementary piece of macroeconomic theory is concerned with the multiplier. The emphasis here is on the market for goods and services. The value of what is supplied in that market equals national income plus imports. The value of what is demanded equals household consumption, government current expenditure on goods and services, investment (public and private), and exports. In the simplest model, all of these except the first are taken as given. Household consumption expenditure is postulated to vary with disposable income, which in turn is taken to be proportionate to national income.

We have, therefore

National Income	Y
+	+
Imports	M
=	=
Consumption	C
+	+
Government Current Expenditure	G
+	+
Investment	I
+	+
Exports	E

If now C is made up of two parts, one dependent on income and one not, we have

$$C = C_1 + C_2$$

C_1 is dependent on disposable income which is proportionate to national income.

Let C_1 equal a fraction, c, of disposable income, which is equal to a fraction, d, of national income.

$$C_1 = cdY$$
$$\therefore C = cdY + C_2$$

Disposable income, is, of course, national income after net taxes are deducted. Therefore, d is equal to $1-t$ where t is the net tax rate (i.e. the tax rate after transfer payments made by the government are netted out).

$$C = c(1-t)Y + C_2$$

If we insert this expression in our basic equation, we have

$$Y + M = c(1-t)Y + C_2 + G + I + E$$

or $$Y = \frac{C_2 + G + I + E - M}{1 - c(1-t)}$$

The mathematical expression $1/\{1-c(1-t)\}$ is called the multiplier. It is the number that non-income related expenditure (or autonomous expenditure) is multiplied by to get national income. Since c is less than one (not all of an increment in income is spent on consumer goods), and t is less than one (not all of an increment in income is taken as taxes), $1 - c(1-t)$ is less than one. It follows that the multiplier is greater than unity.

We can take this argument further. Suppose both imports and exports are made up of two parts:

$$M = M_1 + M_2$$
$$E = E_1 + E_2$$

where M_1 is proportionate to income, and E_1 varies inversely with income. This means that the higher our income, the more we import from abroad and the less we sell abroad.

$$M = mY + M_2$$
$$E = -eY + E_2$$

We can now write national income as

$$Y = \frac{C_2 + G + I + E_2 - M_2}{1 - c(1-t) + e + m}$$

Obviously, the value of the multiplier depends on *c*, *t*, *e*, and *m*. As an example consider the following values:

$$c = 0.9$$
$$t = 0.4$$
$$e = 0.1$$
$$m = 0.4$$

The value of the multiplier would be 1.04.

What this means is that, if government expenditure rose by £1m., national income would rise by £1.04m. Taxes would rise by 40% of that, i.e. £0.42m. Disposable income would rise by 60% of that, i.e. £0.62m. and consumption by £0.56m. Imports would rise by £0.42m. and exports fall by £0.1m. Total home demand for goods and services would rise by £1.56m. (i.e. the increase in consumption plus government current spending). This would be offset by a fall of £0.1m. of sales to foreigners, and of the remainder, £0.42m. would be met by overseas suppliers. It follows that UK national income would rise by only £1.04m. (Note, incidentally, that because tax revenue rises by £0.56m., the government's budgetary position deteriorates by less than the £1m. of increased expenditure.) Lastly, it is necessary to point out that the assumptions we have made for our arithmetic example are rather pessimistic. If *t* were 0.35 and *e* + *m* equal to 0.4, the multiplier would have the larger value of 1.23.

The next step in elementary macroeconomics is to note that investment may depend to some extent on the interest rate. The higher the interest rate, the more costly it is for a firm to add to its stock of productive capital equipment. Thus, given its profits expectations, the less it will be inclined to do so, i.e. its rate of investment will fall. If investment is lower when the interest rate is higher, national income will also be lower. The reason is the one just demonstrated. This inverse relationship between income and the rate of interest is called the IS curve. It is pictured in Figure A.1.

There are three additional points to note about Figure A.1. The first relates to the sensitivity of investment to the rate of interest. The more investment rises for a given fall in the rate of interest, the more income will rise as a consequence. This means that the IS curve will be flatter. Secondly, since we

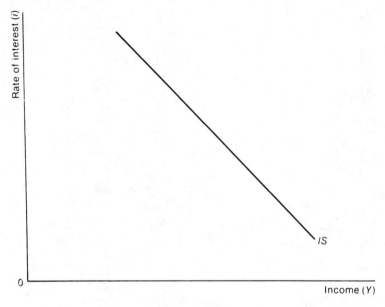

Figure A.1

have postulated that exports fall and imports rise as income rises, the balance of payments on current account deteriorates as we move from left to right along the IS curve. Thirdly, since with I given, income rises if government expenditure rises, the effect of an increase in government expenditure is a rightwards shift in the IS curve. (The size of this shift depends on the size of the multiplier.)

Having raised the question of the interest rate, the next part of the argument in macroeconomics is to ask how the interest rate is determined. One answer is to state that interest is received by holding various assets except money which pays no interest. Another way of putting this is to say that interest is the cost of holding money, in the sense of what has to be given up if a stock of money is to be held. It may be suggested, therefore, that the higher the interest rate, the lower the demand for money to hold.

The reasons for holding money are connected firstly with the transactions that firms and households undertake. These

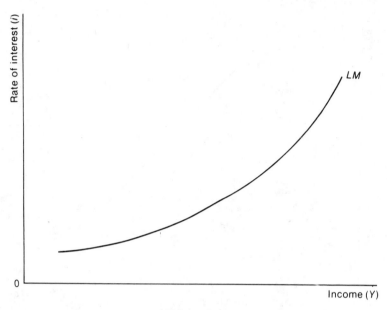

Figure A.2

are reflected in the level of national income. It can be said, therefore, that the higher the level of national income, the higher the demand for money. Money may also be held as an asset to speculate with and the demand for it will depend on the speculative possibilities available, people's attitudes to taking risks, and their expectations of likely gains and losses.

An increase in income will cause an increase in the demand for money. If the supply of money is given, demand will be greater than supply. It must be expected that in the usual way, the price of money will rise, that is the rate of interest will be higher. We have, therefore, an upward sloping relationship between income and the rate of interest. This is called the LM curve, and is pictured in Figure A.2.

There are two further points to note about Figure A.2. The first concerns the sensitivity of the demand for money to the rate of interest and the level of income. The more the demand for money rises as income rises, and the less it falls as the rate of interest rises, the steeper will be the LM curve.

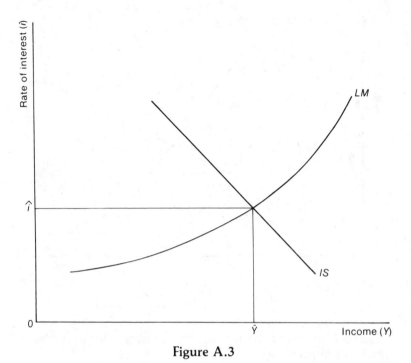

Figure A.3

Secondly, consider what happens if the stock of money were higher. At any level of income the demand for money would be the same. With the supply higher than the demand the rate of interest would fall. In other words, there would be a rightwards shift in the LM curve.

The last step in elementary macroeconomics is to put the two curves together. This is done in Figure A.3.

The IS curve states all combinations of rate of interest and level of income which are compatible with the demand for goods equalling the supply. The LM curve states all combinations of rate of interest and level of income which allow the demand for money to equal the supply. The obvious question is whether there is a combination of i and Y allowing equilibrium in both goods and money markets. This combination must be on both the IS and LM curves, i.e. where they intersect. The point of intersection is shown in Figure A.3, giving

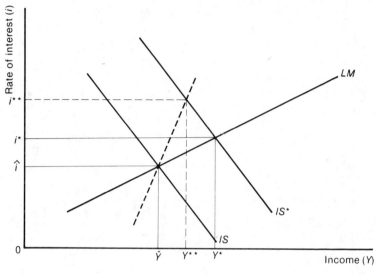

Figure A.4

rise to $\hat{\imath}$ and $\hat{Y}$ as the equilibrium interest rate and level of income, respectively.

The obvious question to ask now concerns possible causes of changes in the equilibrium levels of interest rate and income.

We have already pointed out that an increase in government spending will move the IS curve to the right. It is also the case that an increase in the stock of money will move the LM curve to the right.

Let us take the increase in public expenditure first. The extent to which it shifts the IS curve depends on the size of the multiplier. What happens to national income then also depends on the slope of the LM curve. This is shown in Figure A.4.

The new IS curve is IS*. Given LM, this means that the new equilibrium involves a higher level of income, Y^* greater than $\hat{Y}$, and a higher rate of interest, i^* greater than i. It is also clear that the steeper the LM curve, the more the interest rate will rise and the less income will. A steeper LM curve is illustrated by the dashed line in the figure. Now, we have explained that the steepness of the LM curve depends on the sensitivity of the demand for money to i and Y. In particular, the more sensitive the demand for money is to income and the less sensitive it is to the interest rate, the less an expansionary fiscal policy will raise national income. Instead, it will have a considerable effect on the interest rate, cutting down (or 'crowding out'), that kind of private expenditure affected by the interest rate, i.e. investment.

There are two other points to note about this expansionary policy. We have said that the balance of payments is adversely affected by a rise in income; thus, an increase in government expenditure leads to a fall in exports and a rise in imports. Secondly, in the move from $\hat{Y}$ to Y^* tax revenue will rise but by less than the rise in government expenditure. Therefore, the government's budget position will deteriorate.

(A question in rather more advanced economics is how the government finances its deficit. If it does so by increasing the supply of money, a consequence of the rightward shift of the IS curve will be a further rightward shift of the LM curve. In this way fiscal and monetary actions are intertwined.)

It is now easy to proceed in the same way to examine the consequences of an increase in the stock of money.

It is apparent from Figure A.5 that an increase in the quantity of money which shifts the LM curve to LM* raises national income, but in this case it lowers the interest rate. Moreover, as the dashed line shows, the steeper the IS curve, the less will be the effect on income and the more will be that on the interest rate. The steepness of the IS curve reflects the sensitivity of private investment to the interest rate. The less that sensitivity, the smaller the effect of monetary expansion on income.

Having looked at aggregate demand and at the money market, the next problem to examine concerns the supply of goods and services. This has two sources, home production and overseas.

If home producers are to meet this extra demand, it must be profitable for them to do so. These profits depend on the technical conditions of production and on the costs of variable factors of production, notably wages.

Consider the expansion of output from a low level. Firms

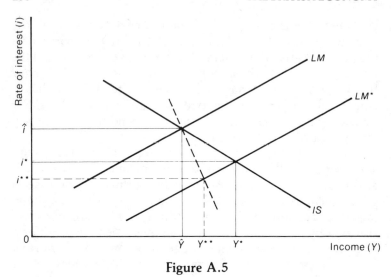

Figure A.5

may have plenty of capital equipment and a good quality and well trained labour force available. No question of diminishing returns arises; there may even be short-run increasing returns. (By this is meant that neither unit nor incremental costs of production will rise as output does.) Eventually, however, as output increases, there may be insufficient equipment to produce it, or the available equipment may be less appropriate and effective. New labour that is taken on may be inferior or in need of special training. Management itself may find it harder to cope with the larger scale of operations. Thus, at a very high level of output, average and marginal productivity may be less than at very low levels of output.

The next consideration to bear in mind is the behaviour of money wages. If income and output are low, and unemployment is higher, the pressure to raise wages will be weak. Confining ourselves to rather static aspects of the subject, it may be suggested that the higher the level of output the higher the level of money wages.

Putting all these thoughts together, the conclusion follows that costs, and therefore prices set, will remain about the same for a whole range of outputs. But beyond a critical level of output, further attempts to increase the scale of operations

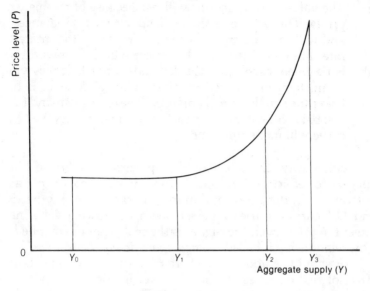

Figure A.6

will push up the price level. This relationship between output and the price level is called the *aggregate supply curve*. It is shown in Figure A.6.

Note that the effect on prices of raising aggregate income from Y_0 to Y_1 is pretty negligible. A further rise to Y_2 does have a significant effect on the price level. Note also that at Y_3 the aggregate supply curve becomes vertical. This means that any attempt to raise output beyond that will fail and be dissipated in higher prices.

Let us now backtrack a little and reconsider the demand for money. The value of money is measured in terms of what it will buy. If the price level doubles, although £100 is still £100, what it will buy is halved. Its *real* value has fallen by a half. Money balances measured relative to the price level are called real balances. It is now easy to see that, if the level of output (and real income) is given, and the price level rises, there will be consequences for the demand for money. This may be looked at in either of two ways:

(i)   The value of transactions will rise because of the higher prices. This will raise the demand for money balances, and with a fixed stock of money, force up the interest rate. In other words, the LM curve will shift upwards.

(ii)   For a given real output, the demand for real balances will be unchanged. The effect of a higher price level is to lower the supply of real balances. The excess demand for real balances will push up the rate of interest, i.e. the LM curve will move upwards.

Either way, the effect of the upwards shift in the LM curve is to reduce real output. In other words, real output as determined in the goods and money markets (i.e. by the IS and LM curves) varies inversely with the price level. The lower the price level, the higher is the real output demanded. This relationship is called the *aggregate demand curve*.

(It should be added that there may also be an important effect of real balances on the IS curve. If prices rise, people with money balances feel worse off. This may cause them to spend less. Thus, C_1 and C_2 may fall, causing income to fall. In other words, a rise in the price level shifts the IS curve to the left as well, reinforcing the leftward shift of the LM curve.)

In Figure A.7 both aggregate demand and aggregate supply curves are shown. Equilibrium occurs at a price level $\hat{P}$ and output level $\hat{Y}$. If aggregate demand rises to AD*, income will rise to Y^* and the price level to P^*. This may result from an increase in government expenditure, or be the result of (say) private investment expenditure resulting from a more optimistic view of the future.

The dashed line shows an alternative aggregate supply curve in which output responds less and the price level more. This may be because productivity deteriorates more, i.e. the economy is nearer to full capacity working. It may also be because wages are pushed up more, because labour is scarcer or trade unions feel stronger.

It is easy to see how the analysis might be used to give an elementary account of inflation and of stagflation.

Let us start by defining a position of full employment, which for our purpopses can be defined as one of maximum

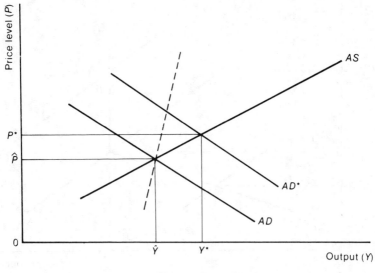

Figure A.7

output. This will be a state of affairs at which the aggregate supply curve becomes vertical. Such a curve is illustrated in Figure A.8.

If AD_0 is the aggregate demand curve, the price level will be P_0 and output will be Y_0. An increase in aggregate demand to AD^* raises the price level to P^* and output to Y^* (i.e. full employment). Any further increases in aggregate demand (e.g. to AD^{**}) causes the price level to rise to P^{**}, but leaves output at Y^*.

It follows that in this example the move to full employment involves some inflation associated with rising output. Having got to full employment, any attempt to raise aggregate demand more still will be entirely inflationary. Thus, the simple answer to what causes inflation, is rising aggregate demand at full employment. Of course, this suggests the necessity of analysing the causes of rising aggregate demand. The obvious points to note are:

(a) They may have their origins in the private or public sectors.

(b) In the private sector there may be an independent in-

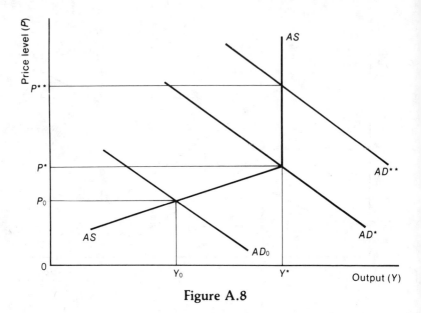

Figure A.8

crease in the propensities to invest, or consume, or export,
any one of which may raise demand relative to maximum
supply.

(c)   In the public sector there may be an increase in govern-
      ment current expenditure on goods and services or
      investment, not matched by a rise in taxes to cut private
      expenditure by the same amount.

We have said that the increase in the private sector may
be independent or autonomous, i.e. it just happens. Equally, if
not more likely, is the possibility that the increased private expenditure is the result of what the government does. If the
government cuts taxes at full employment, the private sector
will have a larger disposable income and will try and spend
more. Thus, the aggregate demand curve rises, but, since output cannot increase, the price level will go up instead.

There is an additional point to bear in mind. If the
government cuts taxes and leaves its own expenditure unchanged, a budget deficit will result. (If there were already a
budget deficit, it will now be larger.) The government has to
finance this deficit and may do so in a way that enlarges the

money supply. We have already pointed out that a rise in the money supply also raises aggregate demand. Thus, the demand pressure is reinforced, making the inflation worse and keeping it going.

Let us now take a different, but related, tack. The price level will rise and go on rising if the aggregate demand curve rises and goes on rising. But the price level will also rise if the aggregate supply curve shifts upwards. One possibility is that something disastrous happens to industry so that its capacity to produce falls. If demand is left alone and capacity to meet it goes down, the price level will rise. This state of affairs may arise as a result of a natural disaster, or of a war which diverts output away from private demand. The effect of the OPEC oil monopoly may also be interpreted in this way. If some of UK output had to be transferred to the oil producers, only the remainder is left to meet UK demand. If UK demand is unchanged, the price level must rise. (It should be added that the rise in the relative price of oil may also render some machinery obsolete or unprofitable to use. The effect of this is to reduce the maximum level of available UK output even more.)

In Figure A.9 the maximum level of output falls to Y^{**}. If aggregate demand is left unchanged, the price level will rise from P^* to P^{**}.

Having looked at aggregate demand and supply separately, let us put the two together. Suppose both curves are shifting upwards. Perhaps the aggregate demand curve is rising because of government deficit finance involving a rising money supply. Perhaps the aggregate supply curve is rising because of continual increases in money wages which raise the prices producers set in order to keep production profitable. (These wage increases may result from a desire on the part of the workers to add to their share of national income or restore levels of real income eroded in the past.)

It is obvious that, if both the aggregate demand and aggregate supply curves rise, the price level will rise as well. It is also clear that if the aggregate supply curve rises more than the aggregate demand curve does, output will fall. This latter example is illustrated in Figure A.10.

We start from a price level P^* and output level Y^*. If

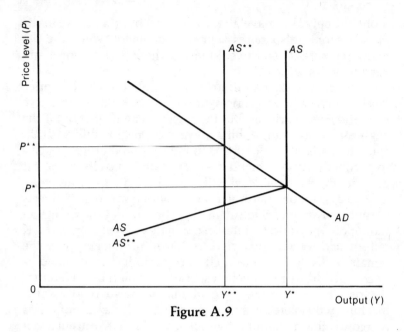

Figure A.9

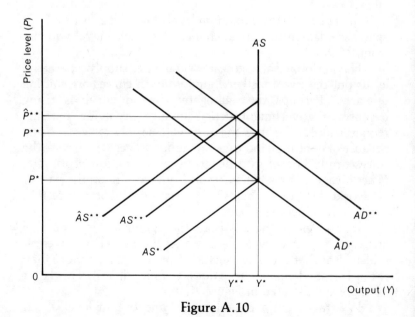

Figure A.10

aggregate demand rises to AD** and aggregate supply to AS**, the price level will rise to P^{**} and output will remain at Y^* (leaving unemployment unaffected). If, however, the aggregate supply curve rises to $\hat{A}S^{**}$, the price level will rise even more still, and output will fall (causing unemployment to rise).

Putting all this together, we can see inflation arising from the joint upward shift of aggregate demand and aggregate supply curves. If the former rises more than the latter, output and employment will also rise unless we are at, or until we reach, full employment. After that only prices will go on rising. If the aggregate supply curve shifts upwards more than aggregate demand, output and employment will fall.

Stagflation may be defined as persistent or rising unemployment in the face of rising prices. It occurs because the aggregate supply curve shifts upwards more than the aggregate demand curve does. (In the simple terms in which we started, this may be put as the result of money wages rising faster than total money demand or the money supply.)

There is one last point to add about all this. The discussion has been concentrated on the elementary static model of macroeconomics. In fact, the typical economy is a growing one. If capacity output increases, aggregate demand can increase by the same amount without inflation occurring. Moreover, the increased capacity to produce, insofar as it is equivalent to a rise in labour productivity, can allow money wages to rise, again without inflation occurring. Thus, all our propositions can be reformulated in dynamic terms. All that is necessary is to substitute for 'rise in aggregate demand (or supply)' the slightly more complicated statement 'rise in aggregate demand (or supply) relative to growth in the economy's underlying capacity to produce'.

Appendix II

The tables in the text are taken from the following publications:

(i)   *Economic Trends Annual Supplement*, 1984 edition.
(ii) *Economic Trends Monthly*, 1984.
(iii) *National Income and Expenditure*, 1983 edition.
(iv) *Department of Employment Gazette*, 1984.
(v) *Annual Abstract of Statistics*, 1984.
(vi) *Bank of England Quarterly Bulletin*, 1984.

The prices of these have risen drastically in recent years, and, presumably, now exceed marginal cost. The result has been to make the task of the teacher of empirical economics much more difficult. The days have long since gone when he could order a copy of the *Blue Book* for every member of class, or ask each of them to buy it for himself.

In the previous edition of this book I pointed out that the increase of the price of the *Blue Book* had far exceeded that of the general level of prices since 1974. In the years since 1980, matters have improved. Prices in general have risen by 24% and the *Blue Book* price by 33%.

The *Bank of England Quarterly Bulletin* is, unhappily, also no longer free. On the assumption that they continue to produce it, it is surprising that they prefer to incur the storage costs of surplus copies, or pulp them, rather than give them away to schools and colleges. Happily, *Economic Progress Report* continues to be available at no charge and is of great value in teaching elementary economics. However, the point about maintaining the critical attitude applies to that as much as to any other publication.

Reference must also be made to the Bank Reviews. These have improved remarkably in recent times. *Lloyds Bank Review* is quite outstanding, as is the *Lloyds Bank Economic Bulletin*. The *Midland Bank Review* is, perhaps, a trifle more difficult, but extremely sound on diagnosis and policy advice. There are also always useful articles in the *Westminster* and *Three Banks Reviews*.

The Economist, although it too has become rather expensive, contains many useful survey pieces. Some of these are directed at the student and the academically-inclined general reader and are most valuable.

On textbooks, I have remarked in the introduction that the best are American (alas). Specially recommended are:

Dornbusch, R. and Fischer, S. (1981) *Macroeconomics*, (2nd edn), McGraw-Hill.
Gordon, R.J. (1984) *Macroeconomics*, (3rd edn), Little Brown.
Parkin, M. and Bade, R. (1982) *Modern Macroeconomics*, Philip Allan.

Their theoretical exposition is excellent. The problem is the emphasis on US experience, and insufficient attention to international aspects of the subject. Dornbusch and Fischer is also a trifle monetarist for my taste, but for the same reason will be especially appealing to some. Parkin and Bade, however, is available in this country in an entirely British edition and is therefore worthy of serious consideration.

Index

Aggregate demand, 155
Aggregate demand curve, 158
Aggregate supply curve, 19, 157

Balance of payments, 79ff., 116, 141, 155
Balance of trade, 3, 145
Barber, 30, 67, 103
Boom, 22, 42, 65, 103

Capital, 46, 55, 123
Capital goods, 11
Capital stock, 34
Competitiveness, 90ff.
Consumer durables, 25
Consumer expenditure, 25ff., 148ff.
Consumer expenditure deflator, 60ff.
Consumer goods, 11
Consumer prices, 73
Credit, 80
Crowding out, 35

Employment, 46ff., 142
Employment, manufacturing, 131ff.
Employment protection, 54
Exchange control, 109
Expectations, 73, 146
Exports, 17, 55, 79ff., 90ff., 148ff.

Factor cost, 8ff.
Fiscal policy, 144
Foreign trade, 2
Full employment, 54, 55, 66, 159-161

Government expenditure, 109ff., 144, 148ff.
Government expenditure deflator, 60ff.
Gross domestic fixed capital formation, 11, 31
Gross domestic product, 6ff., 15ff., 31, 42, 99, 125
Gross domestic product deflator, 58ff.
Gross national product, 6ff.
Growth, 3, 22, 38, 123ff., 142

Healey, 70, 71
Heath, 69, 70, 71, 86

Imports, 79ff., 145, 148ff.
Income from employment, 7
Income from self-employment, 7
Incomes policy, 70ff., 146
Industrial production, 128ff.,
Inflation, 2, 3, 20, 58ff., 104, 142, 144, 145, 159, 163
Interest rate, 150ff.
Investment, 18, 31ff., 93, 130, 148ff.
Investment, foreign, 81
Investment, nationalised industries, 34, 35, 36, 39
Investment, private sector, 34, 35
Investment, public sector, 35
IS curve, 150ff

J-Curve, 85

Kalecki, 2

Keynes, 2, 47

LM Curve, 152ff.

Manufacturing industry, 128ff.
Market, 1, 145
Market prices, 6ff.
Means of payment, 96, 98
Medium of exchange, 96, 98
Monetary policy, 144
Money, 96ff., 161
Multiplier, 19, 148ff.

National income, 6ff., 148ff.
Natural rate of unemployment, 66, 67
North Sea oil, 86, 141

OPEC, 55, 65, 67, 68, 71, 142, 161

Personal disposable income, 14, 27ff.
Phillips curve, 62, 67, 70
Precautionary motive, 97ff.
Prices, 19, 99, 145
Productivity, 131ff.
Profits, 7, 9, 57, 127, 141, 144, 145, 155
Public employment, 113, 120ff.
Public sector borrowing requirement (PSBR),114, 115, 116

Rate of exchange, 82, 88ff., 140
Real money supply, 104, 157
Real terms, 9

Recession, 23, 42, 140
Relative price effect, 64
Rent, 7, 8
Reserves, 82, 84, 88
Retail price index, 1, 58

Saving, 11, 27, 30, 31, 43
Slump, 22
Social security, 48, 54
Speculative motive, 97ff.
Stagflation, 71, 103, 127, 143, 144, 163
Stocks, 12, 38ff.
Supply constraints, 144−145
Supply of labour, 46ff.

Taxation, 46, 109ff., 144, 146
Thatcher, 71
Trades unions, 65, 66, 158
Transactions motive, 97ff.
Transfer payments, 13, 110ff., 144,
Treasury Bills, 114

Unemployment, 1, 2, 3, 45ff., 62, 68, 69, 106ff., 116, 123, 125, 142, 143, 146
Unemployment register, 48ff.

VAT, 72, 109

Wages, 1, 46, 55, 64, 69, 72ff., 87, 94, 106ff., 140, 145, 158, 163
Wages, real, 46−47, 55, 67, 76
Wealth, 98

DATE L I F U R	
08. 12. 86.	29. 0